Fairy Tales, Fables, Legends, and Myths

USING FOLK LITERATURE IN YOUR CLASSROOM

Bette Bosma

TEACHERS COLLEGE, COLUMBIA UNIVERSITY
NEW YORK AND LONDON

Published by Teachers College Press, 1234 Amsterdam Avenue,
New York, N.Y. 10027

Library of Congress Cataloging-in-Publication Data

Bosma, Bette, 1927–
  Fairy tales, fables, legends, and myths.

  Bibliography: p.
  Includes index.
  1. Folk-lore and education. 2. Folk literature—
Study and teaching (Elementary) 3. Reading (Elementary)
4. English language—Composition and exercises.
5. Activity programs in education. I. Title.
LB1583.8.B67 1987   371.3′07′8   86-14570
ISBN 0-8077-2827-6

Manufactured in the United States of America

92 91 90 89 88 87   1 2 3 4 5 6

Fairy Tales, Fables, Legends, and Myths
USING FOLK LITERATURE IN YOUR CLASSROOM

FRONTISPIECE. A Navajo Indian boy enjoys an Italian folktale.

Contents

Preface

I am convinced that teachers make a difference in the development of lifelong readers. A teacher enjoying books, and sharing literature that is interesting for all age levels, stimulates a love of reading and an appreciation of good literature.

This text focuses on folk literature, which is particularly noteworthy for capturing children's interest in reading. In the numerous schools where teachers have been trying the ideas in this book, I have found children from kindergarten to middle school becoming more and more enthralled with the stories.

When a sixth grader helped me take a box of books back to my car, he said, "I wish we could keep them longer. There are still good ones that I haven't had time to read." Before the folk literature study began, this boy had not been able to name five books that he had read on his own.

The teaching ideas and lesson strategies in this book are based on an interactive view of reading. This recognizes the close relationship between reading and writing, and sees them as both processes and skills. Reading is a process of constructing meaning from print, with the reader taking an active role in thinking about the message. The message is interpreted differently by each reader, because each reader brings a unique background to the text.

The communication processes of speaking, listening, reading, and writing work together to produce school learning that translates into learning for real life. Oral responding to the reading is a natural link between the reading and writing.

For more information about integrating reading and writing across the curriculum, consult *Writing and the Writer* by Frank Smith (1982) and *Writing: Teachers and Children at Work* by Donald Graves (1983). For a theoretical explanation of reading as an interactive process, consult Rosenblatt (1978, 1983) or Frank Smith (1978).

Two questions often asked in response to theoretical information about the reading process are: How do we teach reading as a thinking process? How do we foster interaction between the reader, the reading material, and writing? The teaching strategies in this book address these questions. The lessons are adaptable for any grade level, from kindergarten through middle school.

Every teaching idea in this book has been tried with children. I wish to thank the following teachers, who have shared folk literature with their classrooms and have shared the results with me:

Nancy Petersen DeVries, sixth grade reading teacher, J. F. Kennedy Mid School, Gallup, New Mexico.

John Booy, fifth and sixth grade teacher, Beckwith Public School, Grand Rapids, Michigan.

Myra Bradford, fifth and sixth grade reading teacher, Highlands Middle School, Grand Rapids, Michigan.

Maureen Grey, Language Arts consultant, Highlands Middle School, Grand Rapids, Michigan.

Dennis Van Andel and staff at Rehoboth Christian School, Rehoboth, New Mexico, and Calvin College teacher education students who worked in grades kindergarten through six.

Dr. Gaye Voss and staff at Rolling Green Public School, Boynton Beach, Florida, and Calvin College teacher education students.

Nancy Burton, Calvin College graduate student and aide in second and third grade at Stepping Stones Montessori School, Grand Rapids, Michigan.

Mark Van Zanten and Marilyn Scott, first-second grade teachers at Potters House Christian School, Grand Rapids, Michigan.

I would like to thank colleagues who have read the manuscript and encouraged me along the way: Adeline DeBruyn, retired first grade teacher; Kathryn Blok, reading professor at Calvin College; and Helen Bonzelaar, art professor at Calvin College.

Special thanks go to my institution, Calvin College, for approving a sabbatical in which I was able to complete this work.

Fairy Tales, Fables, Legends, and Myths
USING FOLK LITERATURE IN YOUR CLASSROOM

1

Introduction

A rich legacy of folk literature is available to every child. This treasure requires a caring adult to unlock the beauty and enjoyment that the stories contain. The purpose of this book is to acquaint adults with choice folk literature and to provide ideas for sharing these stories with children.

THE IMPORTANCE OF FOLK LITERATURE FOR CHILDREN

Folk literature is worth reading just for fun. The stories contain adventure, humor, and rich language that children can enjoy. In addition, through the folktales, the reader can enter into another culture and recognize the universality of the wishes, dreams, and problems of people around the world. The structure of the tale fulfills the children's expectations. Guided reading of folk literature, directing attention to this story structure, helps the child become a better reader.

Expressive Language

The language of the folk storyteller combines both simple statement and rich, expressive, figurative language. The beauty and richness of language found in authentic written versions of the folktales contributes to children's language development. Folk literature is full of magical language. The magic of words grows in the child who listens to stories. Even before children can produce the words, as listeners they can sense the music of language.

Even the youngest of readers are able to use the predictable narrative patterns to develop an understanding of story ideas and the general meaning of picturesque words. The simple narrative and extensive use of dialogue

1

FIGURE 1.1. A second grader reads a repetitive tale to kindergarten friends.

help in the interpretation of the imagery. If folktales are adapted for easy reading through artificial control, limiting the storyteller's vocabulary and shortening the sentences, the enjoyment and appeal of the language is lost.

In addition, folktales contribute many words and phrases to American speech and literature. These are lost to the person who grows up without a familiarity with folk literature.

The Universality of the Folktale

Folktales help the young reader make sense of the world. Reading different explanations of natural phenomena and ideas clarifies the child's own views. Because folktales have many layers of meaning, readers of differing developmental levels can appreciate them. Teacher guidance enables children to interpret and evaluate the message of the storyteller.

Reading and discussing folk literature enriches the spiritual life of children. They can sense the universal search for a divine being and for answers concerning the origin of the world. A discussion of a powerful legend such as "The Golem" makes children face the relationship between faith and the harsh realities of man's limitations. Folktales demonstrate that people throughout the world share a need for love, hope, and security, and possess feelings of happiness, anger, pride, and loneliness. At the same time, the reader can become sensitive to the differences between cultures. The folk stories show how different peoples respond differently to emotional and environmental conditions.

Folktales possess four characteristics that help the reader assimilate them. First, the magic in the tale lies in people and creatures being shown as they really are, not as results of wishes or dreams. In fact, wishes usually are shown to be foolish, as in "The Fisherman and His Wife," in which the wife's discontent causes her to lose all she gained by wishing. Second, natural wit, intelligence, and goodness generally outsmart evil, as in Molly Bang's *Wiley and the Hairy Man,* in which the brave Wiley outwits the wicked Hairy Man. Third, the magical power is limited. It cannot change a heart or the state of the world, but only outward conditions. Cinderella's clothes and conditions are changed, not her personality or character. Finally, evil does not win, but receives its due or is recognized as evil. Sometimes this includes a harsh treatment of evil, such as in Glo Coalson's version of "Three Stone Woman."

Children who have a good sense of story structure have formed expectations for the role of characters. Nine-year-olds respond to the question, "What is a _____ usually like?" with the reply that a wolf is hungry, a fox is sly, a witch is wicked, or a fairy is kind (Applebee, 1978, p. 50).

Folktale characters are drawn very clearly and generally depicted as symbols of good or evil, wisdom or foolishness, power or weakness. This polarization of characters fits into the children's expectations, which have been developing since age two, through both realistic and fanciful stories. Bruno Bettelheim (1976) argues that this stock characterization helps the child comprehend the differences between reality and fantasy more readily than is possible when figures are drawn true to life. The ambiguity that characterizes real people is difficult for a child to comprehend until the child has established positive self-identification.

FOLKLORE CLASSIFICATIONS AND DEFINITIONS

Two kinds of folklore classifications have received universal use. Antti Aarne, a Finnish folklorist, developed a *type index* in 1910. This index assigns a type number to each tale. For example, "Cinderella" is Type 510. Stith

Thompson, folklorist from Indiana University, published a *motif index* in 1932. This breaks each tale into small units and assigns a motif number to each unit of action and each character or major subject within the tale. For example, number R221, "flight from ball," lists "Cinderella" as a tale that includes that motif. This *Motif-Index of Folk Literature*, currently published in six volumes, is accepted by folktale scholars around the world as a standard tool for classifying folktale materials.

In *The Storyteller's Sourcebook: A Subject, Title, and Motif Index to Folklore Collections for Children* (1982), Margaret Read MacDonald has made a significant contribution to folk literature for children. This source includes all folktale titles that appeared in the editions of the *Children's Catalog* published between 1971 and 1981, and indexes 556 folktale collections and 389 picture books. In addition to the motif index, which is useful for finding tale variants, the source contains a tale title index, subject index, and ethnic and geographic index. This enables the teacher, librarian, or child to find tales about a given subject, the location of the collection that contains a particular story, or titles of tales from a particular ethnic or geographic area.

Folklorists and users of folklore do not always agree on definitions and classifications of the various tales. The one area of agreement is recognition that folk literature originates in the oral tradition. The stories were passed along by storytellers and then became literature when written down by a person who heard and interpreted the tale. That person is labeled the collector, translator, adapter, or reteller of the folktale.

The child reader deserves to be introduced to folk literature in as authentic a representation as possible. Therefore, the classifications and criteria developed in this book follow the standards of the American Folklore Society. The definitions are based on descriptions found in the *Standard Dictionary of Folklore, Mythology, and Legend* (Leach & Freed, 1949).

Folktale is an inclusive term, referring to all kinds of narrative that has its origin in the oral tradition. The *literary folktale*, or *folk literature*, is the tale translated and retold based upon the storytelling characteristic of a particular cultural group.

Four types of folktales are identified throughout this book: *fairy tales, animal tales, legends,* and *myths.* These four were chosen because they encompass the vast majority of the tales in print today for children, and because they are fairly distinctive in their differences. Each types is defined and explained in this section.

Fairy Tales

A fairy tale is an unbelievable tale that includes an enchantment or supernatural elements that are clearly imaginary. It does not necessarily contain fairies, but often has giants or witches as well as brave and timid, good and evil people. Such stories are also referred to as household tales (the German Märchen, or "wonder tales"). Fairy tales share characteristics, but not every fairy tale contains all the distinctive characteristics. Fairy tales:

> show how people behave in a world of magic
> often have brave heroes who rescue a helpless maiden
> contain some characters who are either all good or all bad
> often begin with "Once upon a time" and end with "Happily ever after" or a similar convention
> often include a task, which, if completed, brings a reward
> often include a magic object to protect or help the main character

Animal Tales

The animal tale is one of the oldest forms of folk literature and is found everywhere on the globe. The primary characters are animals who act like people. These stories teach about life, usually with lessons concerning personal traits and getting along with others. There are three main categories of animal tales: trickster or beast tales, fables, and etiological (why or pourquoi) stories.

Trickster tales contain one central character, usually a wise trickster in animal shape. In some cultures, the animal character will assume a human shape at times. Anansi, the spider of African origin, is an old man in some stories or a young man in tales from the Antilles. Trickster tales are usually brief and direct. The story relies on one action, a trick or joke, as the solution to the problem. However, this is not a simple solving of a problem. The climax of a trickster tale must be an unusual solution requiring admirable mental prowess. The story ends in a clever way, often with a surprising element that entertains or amuses the reader. The special quality of the ending makes the trickster tale memorable.

Various cultural groups name a specific animal hero. The hare, a symbol of wisdom, is named Zomo in Africa, Br'er Rabbit in the southern United

States, and Manabozho by the Indians of the southwestern United States. Other distinctive animal tricksters include the spider in West Africa and the Antilles, Coyote among Indian tribes of the northwestern United States and Canada, Raven among Innuits and Indians of the Northwest, Fox in Russia, and the turtle, terrapin, or tortoise in North and West Africa and among the Indians of the southwestern United States.

Fables are brief animal stories with a specific lesson, generally stated at the beginning or end. Often one animal depicts the good traits and one depicts the evil. The animals are not named or developed beyond the single purpose of the tale. The fable appears to be a simple tale, but the compressed narrative reveals many layers of meaning. Two major collections of fables are the Jataka tales from Eastern culture and Aesop's fables from Western culture.

Jataka tales, recorded as early as 500 B.C., are moralistic lessons in which the Buddah is reincarnated as one of several animals, generally a lamb, deer, or crane. The philosophy taught in the Jataka tales involves recognizing the importance of the individual and the need to accept and understand the realities of life. Traits of cooperation, friendship, respect, ecology, and responsibility are emphasized. In English translations many of the morals and teaching verses are eliminated.

Aesop's fables are associated with a Greek slave, Aesop, who allegedly lived in Asia Minor about 600 B.C. The lessons of Aesop's fables are directed toward manipulating external forces and controlling or overcoming enemies.

Etiological, or *pourquoi,* animal tales explain the origin of certain characteristics of animals and were written to entertain. In contrast to legend, the pourquoi tales were not believed to be true. One can find many explanations for why the bear has a stumpy tail or why mosquitoes buzz in people's ears. The element of trickery is essential to the plot of this form of animal tale. The pourquoi form is often emulated by authors of invented stories, such as Rudyard Kipling with his famous "Just So" stories.

Legends

Legends are folktales told as fact and presumably believed by the storyteller. They are set in a historic time and place, in a recognizable world. The nature of the tale can be sacred or secular, often concerned with changes in creation, transformation of humans and animals, or heroic deeds. A legend can be explanatory or historical. The principle characters are humans, animals acting like humans, and supernatural creatures. A legend will often state a natural or historical fact, and then proceed to prove the fact by drawing erroneous conclusions. People in legend are concerned about the results of the conflict of natural phenomena.

Legendary characters have their origin among the folk, handed down in the oral tradition. In contrast, some alleged American folk heroes have been deliberately invented. Consequently, stories about these heroes are classified as modern fantasy rather than folk literature. Paul Bunyan was created in 1914 by an advertising man, W. B. Laughhead, as a promotion figure for the Red River Lumber Company. Pecos Bill, a legendary cowboy, and Joe Magarac, a steelworker, were both invented by magazine writers in the early 1900s. Although the name Johnny Appleseed originated from a real person, John Chapman, the attributes credited to him and incidents related in the Johnny Appleseed stories were fabricated.

Myths

Myths are folktales told as fact that develop a theory of the origin of the world and of man. Myths are set in a remote past, in which gods lived on the earth and humans had not yet developed an understanding of the arts and customs of life. The nature of the tale is sacred, concerned with the creation of the world and origins of natural events. The principal characters are deities and supernatural powers, often with human attributes. In some cultures, myths and legends are combined into one category since both types of tales are presumed true by historic storytellers. The Native Americans maintain a clear distinction between these two types of folktales, based primarily on setting.

TRANSLATION OF FOLK LITERATURE

Folk literature could not be enjoyed by American readers if the stories had not been translated. In fact, the only tales that originated in English are the American regional and tall tales. American Indian myths and legends were first told or written down in tribal language. Increased interest in folklore in the 1980s has encouraged many people to translate old tales into English for the first time.

Authentic translation requires considerable study. For example, John Bierhorst, a well-respected adapter of American Indian tales, translated *The Spirit Child* into English in 1984 from Aztec Indian documents of the mid

1500s. Ai-Ling Louie studied manuscripts that date back to A.D. 618–907 before translating *Yen Shen* into English. Lynette Dyer Vuong studied several Vietnamese folktale volumes before attempting her colorful translation of *The Brocaded Slipper and Other Vietnamese Tales* in 1982. Boris Zvorykin translated four Russian fairy tales into French as a gift of gratitude for the new life he made in France in the 1920s after the Russian Revolution. The fairy tales were translated into English in 1978, and published with reproductions of the original illustrations. Verna Aardema investigates as many early translations of old African scripts as possible before beginning her versions of African tales. She incorporates ideophones from the African language to add rhythm and flavor to the story.

The reader or teller of tales can increase children's awareness that the folktales they enjoy are translated from other languages. Whenever introducing or sharing a folktale, tell the children, or ask them to discover, the original language of the story. References found in book prefaces or epilogues can stimulate children to embark on individual inquiries, researching the country, the language, or the act of translating.

The fifth-sixth grade class discussed in chapter six was asked, "What if no one had translated these stories? Would that make a difference to you?" Typical answers were:

> I'd miss the fun of reading them.
> If we read their stories [those belonging to other cultures] and like them we will cooperate more with them because we will see that we agree with each other.
> We wouldn't learn how different people from different places teach their children. When we read them it teaches us lessons just like they taught their children lessons.
> They are of great value because they teach us why things are important and why things are the way they are.

PREVIEW

In the following chapters lessons are presented to help adults share the books with children. The goal of every lesson is to heighten the appreciation of the stories and the ability to read. The lessons should be viewed as examples, not as prescriptions, and the teacher should adapt ideas from the model to fit a particular class. The lists of folktales presented are by no means exhaustive. Other literary tales may be used with any of the teaching ideas.

Children who learn to read through folk literature have the opportunity to become lifetime readers, understand other people, and appreciate other cultures. The teachers who have been involved in trying the teaching ideas presented here have expressed a new excitement for reading, both for themselves and their pupils.

2

Understanding the Story

A classroom study of folk literature should begin with storytelling or reading the tales aloud. The group of children listening to and watching the storyteller follows the oral tradition begun before print was invented. Cultural groups around the world developed storehouses of tales that were told in family and clan gatherings to entertain, to explain the world around them and to caution and teach the young.

The magic of the story is captured in the telling, and most children need this introduction before they will enjoy reading the stories themselves. Teachers in a middle school who used folk literature in their reading program reported that reading one folktale a day, or one that took two days to complete, whetted the pupils' interest. Frequently the children would select those stories to reread.

READING ALOUD

When reading folktales aloud, teachers should take time to stop and discuss interesting ideas, cultural differences, and the storyteller's rich use of language. The beauty and richness of language found in authentic versions of folktales contribute to children's language development. You can direct the oral reading experience by reading aloud for language response and for predictions.

Reading Aloud for Language Response

A kindergarten or first grade teacher cannot assume that all children will come to school knowing nursery tales such as "Three Billy Goats Gruff," "Gingerbread Boy," "Henny-Penny," or "The Little Red Hen." Children who do know them delight in hearing these favorite stories again and again. Many of the folktales that please the very young child use a repetitive or a cumulative story pattern. The repetitive pattern is characterized by a refrain or an episode being repeated. The cumulative pattern adds a new thought or episode, and then repeats what has gone before in the story. Both patterns enhance the young child's awareness of language. Young children delight in discovering a pleasing flow of language, and in being able to repeat the rhythmical expressions. The rhythmical pattern helps the child understand and recall the sequence and the content of the story. The framework directs the reader's attention to the next episode and helps him keep track of what has happened. When simpler words are substituted, but the anticipated patterns are broken, the story is made more difficult rather than easier to understand.

The superb telling of the nursery tales by Paul Galdone uses repetition of words and phrases. The following plan utilizes this repetition to provide both enjoyment and language growth.

LESSON OBJECTIVE: To develop language awareness through repetition of phrases in an enjoyable story.

MATERIAL: One of Paul Galdone's books (see chapter seven) or another folktale with a repetitive pattern; tagboard strips with the printed refrain from the story.

PROCEDURE:

1. Read the story expressively.
2. After the refrain has been repeated a few times, stop just short of the next time it occurs. Ask the children to join you. If they do not respond, simply continue reading, but give auditory emphasis to the refrain.
3. The next time the refrain is repeated, stop and nonverbally indicate that the listeners may provide the next words. With some groups, this will begin spontaneously. Others will need more modeling before they are free to respond.
4. Reread the story either at the same sitting or at another time, and place the tagboard strips in a pocketchart. This provides a speech-to-print correspondence for the nonreader, and a printed version for the beginning reader. Resist the urge to use the tagboard strip at the first reading. The children who know the speech-to-print relationship will benefit, but the ones who have not yet developed that concept will not.

5.   Variations of step four can involve child participation in placing the strips or reading them. Make sure that the child who needs to develop this prereading concept is an active participant.

Language patterns assist experienced readers as well as beginners. Folktales such as "Tikki Tikki Tembo," "Why Mosquitoes Buzz in People's Ears," "Strega Nona," and "Bringing the Rain to Kapiti Plain" contain repetitive and cumulative patterns. When reading these and similar tales, elicit response from the listeners to emphasize language patterns.

Reading Aloud for Predictions

Asking children to predict what they think the story will be about engages them as active participants. As the story unfolds, the listeners are able to stick to or change their predictions. This establishes a purpose for reading and a thoughtful approach to understanding the story.

LESSON OBJECTIVE: To encourage listeners to predict the turn of events in the story and to recognize the need for information in making a valid prediction.

MATERIAL: Since all folktales are predictable to varying degrees, select a tale that fits the level of thinking of your children.

Examples for primary grades: *The Summer Maker* or *The First Morning: An African Myth* by Margery Bernstein and Janet Kobrin, *Who's in Rabbit's House?* by Verna Aardema, *Fin M'Coul* by Tomie dePaola.

Examples for intermediate grades: *The Dancing Granny* by Ashley Bryan, *Three Stone Woman* by Glo Coalson, *Liang and the Magic Paintbrush* by Demi, *The Long-tailed Bear* by Natalie Belting.

PROCEDURE:

1.   Read the story aloud and elicit predictions, beginning with the title, or the opening sentences.
2.   Stop reading at a planned spot, and ask if any predictions have already come true, or if the listeners want to change a prediction. If they wish to change, expect them to give their reasons, based on what they have heard so far in the story.
3.   Ask the listeners to respond to such questions as:
     a.   Why don't you know if your prediction is true?
     b.   What other information do you need?
     c.   Do you want to keep your prediction, or change it? Why?

After the children become adept at making and verifying predictions from folktales, guide prediction practice with other types of writing, such as news stories and editorials. This will help readers understand that what they learn from story reading is applicable to other kinds of literature.

GENERAL COMPREHENSION

Full appreciation of stimulating folktales comes when the reader can understand the story while reading silently. The teacher's role is to make these stories available, in the classroom or library, and to guide the readers toward an understanding of what they read.

Folktales can be used with all ages of children because of the tales' many layers of meaning. The subtle messages that delight the older child are not picked up by the younger reader, but that does not lessen the latter's appreciation of the story. The experienced teacher adjusts the lessons to challenge children at their appropriate developmental level. For example, consider the different responses given by primary school children and older intermediates to *Baba Yaga* by Ernest Small. The younger child expects Marusia to get away from the witch because of the predictability of the fairy tale: children always escape the witch! The older child responds to the theme and expects Marusia to be released because of the message: evil cannot win in the presence of love. A teacher must strive for a balance that avoids either making a lesson too easy or assuming that the children have more knowledge than they really do.

For some of the strategies described in this chapter, alternatives for different age levels are given, but generally that decision must be left to the discretion of the teacher. Two methods for guiding silent reading are described: story mapping and the directed reading-thinking activity.

Story Mapping

A story map is a graphic display of the logical organization of events and ideas important in the unfolding of the story. Use of story mapping develops comprehension by directing the reader's attention to the story structure.

The teacher must become proficient at mapping stories before introducing the process to children. During preparation for group mapping the teacher should devise questions that will aid the reader in organizing and integrating the story content, and should avoid questions that simply test recall or focus on literal meaning. Questions should consider the overall concept of the story rather than isolated items in it.

TEACHER PREPARATION FOR STORY MAPPING

1. Select a simple folktale that the children have heard or read, such as *Fin M'Coul,* for the first mapping experience.
2. Fill in map (see figure 2.1) while reviewing the story.
3. Generate questions from the sequence of the story, such as:
   a. "When does the author tell you the problem?" In some stories, the problem is stated after an elaborate introduction. With folktales, the problem is usually stated quickly and simply, making these stories excellent to use as the first models for group story mapping.
   b. "Why did you call that an action?" Expect the children to give a reason for their answers. Selecting main actions as opposed to details is the skill used here, and the reader should be made aware of how the answer fits or does not fit into the structure.
   c. "When did you realize the problem was being solved?" Include "what

FIGURE **2.1.** Story mapping chart.

```
TITLE OF STORY


SETTING          Where
                 When

CHARACTERS       Who


PROBLEM


ACTION           1

                 2

                 3   (as many as needed)


RESOLUTION
```

if" questions if you wish to discuss alternative ways of solving the problem.

4. Decide which questions should be asked before the story is read and which should be asked while mapping. The question "What is the problem?" can be answered as soon as that identifying part is read. Ask this after reading. The question, "How does the trickster solve the problem?" is not answered until the end of the story. Ask questions like this before reading.

INTRODUCING STORY MAPPING TO CHILDREN

LESSON OBJECTIVE: To help children recognize the structure of a story.
MATERIAL: The folktale that you have selected; chart paper or newsprint; story map outlines for individuals (optional).
PROCEDURE:

1. Reproduce the story map outline on a large piece of newsprint, so that it is visible for all. (See figure 2.2.) Each child can have a copy to fill out while the teacher is writing on the large chart.
2. While filling out the map, the pupils should be involved in answering questions about setting and characters. When time or place is not stated, inferential thinking is needed. Demonstrate how clues to determining setting can be picked up through pictures, dialogue, or particular phrases. For the first mapping experience with young children, select a story that gives all the setting information very clearly. Note how Tomie dePaola begins his retelling of *Fin M'Coul:*
   > In olden times,
   > when Ireland's glens and woods
   > were still filled with fairies and leprechauns,
   > giants, too lived on that fair Emerald Isle. (p. 1)

   Here you have all the information concerning setting in the opening lines.
3. The teacher continues to guide, discussing how to state the problem as simply as possible, and selecting the actions. At first the teacher should say why each action is chosen. Then, once the children recognize that each action must work toward solving the problem, they can say why each action is chosen. The teacher can demonstrate that by comparing the contributing actions with minor episodes that do not advance the story line.

FIGURE 2.2
Fourth graders map a story they have read with their teacher.

4. Guide the reader to state the resolution in key words chosen from the story.

Several modeling experiences may be necessary before the readers can use story mapping as a tool for better understanding of the story. Moving from teacher-led mapping to small groups, to partners, and then to independent mapping makes the experience more enjoyable and provides the necessary practice.

Directed Reading-Thinking Activity

A second strategy for guiding readers to general comprehension is the directed reading-thinking activity (Stauffer, 1980). This activity is similar to the strategy used in the reading-aloud-for-predictions lesson, but now the child reads silently. The predict-read-prove sequence gives a purpose for reading and engages the reader in thinking about the broad and deep meaning of the story content. The practice in making predictions while listening prepares the reader for making predictions before and during silent reading.

FIGURE 2.3. Second grade partners plan a story map.

LESSON OBJECTIVE: To guide readers to general comprehension.

MATERIAL: Multiple copies of a folktale that pupils can read. (Many basal readers have adaptations of folktales that would be appropriate for this activity.)

PROCEDURE:

1. Meet with a small group of pupils.
2. Predict—elicit predictions based on the title and pictures.
3. Read—ask pupils to read to a certain point.
4. Prove—discuss whether or not the predictions are coming true, and whether more information is needed.
5. Continue this sequence, with teacher-selected stopping places for discussion.

VOCABULARY DEVELOPMENT

Words must communicate a message to the listener or reader in order to be understood and remembered. New vocabulary grows through new experiences, and the use of language to describe these new experiences. Literature plays an important role here, because as children listen and respond to stories, they extend both their experiential background and their exposure to new language.

Two vocabulary strategies are described in this section: the use of oral and written context, and the understanding of figurative language.

Oral and Written Context

Able readers enrich their vocabularies greatly in independent reading by interpreting new words in context. Teachers can guide young readers to develop the habit of scrutinizing the context of unfamiliar words and phrases so that the reader can make sensible guesses, or predictions, about the meaning of the unknown words.

Vocabulary consists of various kinds of language:

> *plot-carrying words,* which must be known in order to understand the story line
>
> *descriptive words,* which indicate the author's style and set the mood
>
> *concept-carrying words,* which require adequate background knowledge for understanding the theme of the story

While children usually experience little difficulty with plot-carrying and descriptive words, they may need help with concept-carrying words. Difficult concept-carrying words will need prior explanation, or may be an indication that the tale is more appropriate for older children. For example, cautionary tales often deal with character traits. Many of those tales use humor to get the message across to the reader. *The Lazies* by Mirra Ginsburg was a favorite of sixth graders who were studying folktales. To truly enjoy the humor, the reader had to know the meaning of such words as *shrewdness, laziness,* and *idler.* When children respond to a story by saying, "I didn't get it," or "The story doesn't make sense," it means they generally are unable to understand the concept-carrying vocabulary.

In the same sixth grade, many children were attracted to Jan Carew's *The Third Gift.* However, few would finish it. Finally, one boy brought it to his teacher and asked if she would read it to the class, because it seemed so good, but was hard to understand. The teacher read it, stopping frequently to ask the listeners what a particular phrase meant, such as, "Through endless seasons of waxing and waning moons" (p. 10). When the sixth graders heard the expressions in context, they were able to understand them. The difficult language was easier to understand because now, in addition to the written context, the listener could use cues of intonation, stress, pitch, and juncture to help conceptualize the meaning. The discussions that followed demonstrated a rich understanding and appreciation for the life views of the Juba people. Analyzing the context helped the reader interpret the message.

LESSON OBJECTIVE: To help the reader unlock the message by making sensible guesses from the context.

MATERIAL: *The Third Gift* by Jan Carew; transparencies and overhead projector.

PROCEDURE:

1. After reading *The Third Gift* aloud, show the following difficult passage on an overhead projector.

   > Amakosa summoned the elders of the clan to a palaver. It was a time when endless seasons of drought and dust were scattering the Jubas. (p. 7)

   Lead the students in analyzing why they were not able to understand this.

   a. What didn't you understand when you tried to read this alone? (Underline those words not grasped.)

   b. What made it possible to understand it when you heard it?

2. If all the responses lead to the oral communication, point out that written messages can be harder to understand because there are less clues for finding the meaning. Then demonstrate how the reader can examine the other words in the passage. Draw arrows to the words, and suggest questions that the reader should ask himself to determine the meaning. For example, if *palaver* is the unknown word, underline it on the transparency and ask the following questions:

   a. Do the surrounding words tell you enough for you to guess the meaning of the unknown word?

   b. If not, what should you do: skim to find *palaver* in another sentence and try again, or look it up in the dictionary?

3. Present a new passage on the transparency, such as:

   > One evening, when the gloaming was giving way to starlight and pale lightnings . . . (p. 10)

   Lead readers to verbalize what they would look for and think about when deciding on the meaning of the passage. Repeat the process used with *palaver,* asking which word to underline and where to draw arrows for supporting clues. Suggest that the reader say a difficult passage quietly aloud if oral clues help.

4. Allow silent reading time during which the readers are encouraged to notice what they do when they read a word or idea that is not clear. Take time to discuss their findings.

As a reinforcing activity, post a chart in the room on which children can write unusual words in the context in which they found them.

Folktales that have been retold with the flavorful language of the native country introduce children to many literary words that they would not hear in other settings. If interest in language has been developed, children will be able to understand the unusual words from the context, and simple easy-to-read versions will not be necessary.

Figurative Language

The young reader needs to understand idiomatic and figurative expressions. Understanding figurative language leads children to create their own fresh metaphors, and make better use of learned, or frozen, metaphors. Similes, metaphors, and idioms are found in nearly every child's story, both in basal readers and in children's literature. Unless this figurative speech is taught, children tend to misunderstand the message of the author.

Common idioms used by a particular group are difficult for the child from a different cultural background, and for the child who comes from a home where the family seldom converses together. The idiom of folktales from other countries will be new to most children and offer a common ground to begin teaching how to interpret idioms.

LESSON OBJECTIVE: To recognize idioms as expressions peculiar to a language or dialect of a region or class of people, with a meaning different from the literal; to be able to interpret idioms in independent reading.

MATERIAL: *When Shlemiel Went to Warsaw and Other Stories* by Isaac Bashevis Singer; transparencies; chart paper.

PROCEDURE:

1. Read "Shrewd Todie and Lyser the Miser" for enjoyment (p. 3).
2. Explain that much of the humor in the story depends on understanding the idioms. If necessary, define *idiom* and introduce it as a new word to be remembered.

3. Show the prepared transparency with an idiom from the story:
   It was said of Todie that if he decided to deal in candles the sun would never set. (p. 3)
4. Discuss what the literal meaning would be: What clues about the literal meaning help you decide on the intended meaning?
5. Note that idioms can be categorized by their main source of comparison: animals, color, clothing, food, plants, solar system, or parts of the body. Decide on the category for that idiom. Compare the meaning within that category to the context of the idiom.

For a reinforcing activity, prepare a chart with the names of possible categories for the source of the idiom. Encourage the children to categorize idioms that they meet in their reading, using steps 4 and 5 to guide them.

Metaphors and similes can be taught in a similar manner. Similes are the easiest to understand, since the clue words *like* or *as* are used, and young children can be taught to understand and use similes effectively. Metaphors, with the implied comparison, are more difficult to understand, and children often get incorrect visual pictures because of this misunderstanding. Lifting these phrases out of a story and examining them together orally leads children to enjoy those expressions rather than skip over them. Such direct instruction in figurative language exerts a powerful influence on children in developing their own understanding and use of idioms, similes, and metaphors.

Sixth graders offered the following written explanations for figurative expressions that they found in their independent folktale reading:

> He's a wolf in sheep's clothing (from Aesop's fables). Child's explanation: He's like a private agent.
> Don't count your chickens before they hatch (from Aesop's fables). Children's explanations: —Like, you're mowing a lawn and you have the money spent before you get it. —Like, my sister had 5 kittens and five people who wanted them. Then one died.
> My heart is breaking with grief (from *Loon's Necklace*). Child's explanation: I'm so sad that there's a lump in my throat.

SUMMARY

An enthusiastic and knowledgeable teacher can enhance pupils' understanding of the story in numerous ways. Teaching strategies in this chapter are designed to assist the teacher in helping children enjoy and appreciate stories. Suggestions for reading aloud include reading for language response and for predictions. Guiding silent reading includes eliciting predictions through a directed reading-thinking activity and mapping based on the structure of the story. Vocabulary lessons focus on the oral and written context of the unknown word or phrase and figurative language interpretation.

3

Critical Reading

The child who becomes a lifelong reader is one who has developed an appreciation for reading. Appreciation is enhanced by the ability to read critically. Critical reading is a process of reconstructing the meaning of the printed message through analysis, synthesis, and evaluation. It is a complex skill that requires direct instruction, practice, and experience, plus the ability to sustain a questioning attitude toward the narrative. The ability to read critically should become as much a part of the reading act as general comprehension or word recognition. The goal of teaching critical reading is to develop a discerning reader, not a literary critic.

Folktales provide excellent stories for the teacher to read while modeling critical reading skills. Because they are multileveled, they can be interpreted at a level appropriate to the reader. They follow predictable stories that the reader can follow with ease. Therefore, with proper guidance from the teacher, children can direct their thoughts beyond the printed work to interpreting and evaluating the message of the storyteller.

Lessons in this section are models for teaching four specific critical reading skills. The procedure used with these four skills can be adapted for any other aspect of critical reading that you wish to teach. The skills developed here are the ability to classify, the ability to compare relevant information and draw conclusions from those comparisons, the ability to make judgements based on clearly defined standards, and the ability to recognize the theme of a story and to evaluate the effectiveness of the presentation of the theme. These skills need not be taught in the order presented. Although thinking-reading skills are interrelated, one does not have to be mastered in order for the the reader to understand the other.

CLASSIFYING TYPES AND CHARACTERISTICS

Classifying folktales gives the reader a framework for learning how to categorize ideas into groups and subgroups. Folk historians and users do not agree on folktale classifications. Many stories include elements of both legend and myth, or some element of fairy tale. Animals are main characters in much folklore—not only in that classified as animal tale. This very arbitrary nature of the categorizing makes folk literature appropriate for using with readers who are developing the skill of recognizing similar characteristics and using that skill to group ideas. Teaching suggestions are given for developing the background necessary for categorizing fairy tales, animal tales, legends, and myths.

Fairy Tales

LESSON OBJECTIVE: To introduce fairy tales.

MATERIALS: "Vassilissa the Fair" (*The Firebird,* by Boris Zvorykin, p. 63) is a good tale to use for modeling by teachers in grades four through six with children who already know Cinderella. It is a Russian version of Cinderella, with added motifs that demonstrate all the characteristics of a good fairy tale. For the younger child, a version of Perrault's *Cinderella* will be the most familiar story.

PROCEDURE:

1. Read the story for sheer enjoyment of the tale. Then, present the following characteristics by making a statement and asking clarifying questions, or by eliciting the statement from the students, based on their listening to the story of Vassilissa. While discussing each statement, present the following points on a poster or with an overhead projector.
   Fairy tales:
   a. show how people behave in a world of magic
   b. often have brave heroes who rescue a helpless maiden
   c. contain some characters who are either all good or all bad
   d. often begin with "Once upon a time" and end with "Happily ever after"
   e. often include a task, which, if completed, brings a reward
   f. often include a magic object to protect or help the main character
2. The following questions assist in eliciting thoughtful answers from the pupils:
   a. Who was human in this story?

b. Was there a brave hero? Explain. (Vassilissa is a brave heroine, and a discussion will probably ensue as to whether or not the czar was a hero in this story.)

c. Were some characters all good and some all bad? Explain your choice.

d. What was the task and the reward?

e. Did any event happen three times? Was there a special reason for this number?

f. What was the importance of the magic object, the doll?

g. Does this story give you any insights about the Russian people?

The characteristics can be posted in the room, or individual copies given to the children so they can refer to them while finding these elements in stories they read on their own.

Familiar fairy tales as well as less common tales should be available in the classroom. The wide variety will make it possible for children to select a tale at their own reading level and to fulfill their need for either familiarity or challenge. The children's independent reading should be followed by a sharing time during which they discuss what they read and how their story fit the fairy tale characteristics.

Animal Tales

A fable is an animal story with a specific lesson, generally stated at the beginning or end. Examples described in chapter seven include *Aesop's Fables, The Jataka Tales, The Fables of La Fontaine,* and *Once upon a Mouse* by Marcia Brown.

Trickster, or beast, stories contain one central character, usually a trickster in animal shape. Trickster stories described in chapter seven include *The Tiger and the Rabbit* by Pura Belprè, *Anansi the Spider* by Gerald McDermott, *Coyote Tales* by Hettie Jones, and *Zomo the Rabbit* by Hugh Sturton.

Pourquoi tales explain certain specific phenomena dealing with animals, such as why the bear lost his tail or why the leopard has spots. Typical stories described in chapter seven include *Why Mosquitoes Buzz in People's Ears* by Verna Aardema, *Dance of the Animals* by Pura Belprè, and *Cherokee Animal Tales* by George Scheer.

Animal tales include three subcategories: fables, trickster stories and pourquoi tales.

LESSON OBJECTIVE: To introduce animal stories.
MATERIAL: Any of the stories mentioned above.
PROCEDURE: The same format can be used with animal tales as was used with fairy tales, following five steps:
1. Read a story for enjoyment.
2. State the characteristics of animal tales.
   a. Main characters are animals who act like people.
   b. The stories teach about life, usually lessons concerning personal traits and getting along with others.
3. Elicit response from the children finding the characteristics in the model tale.
4. Children read individual tales, noting the similarity and differences from the model tale.
5. Share experiences of reading the individual stories.

Legends and Myths

The difference between legends and myths is not easy to discern. The teacher can use either the direct format outlined with the other categories and teach legends and myths separately, or teach by comparing the myth and the legend. With some groups, modeling each category separately, and then comparing (before the children are asked to attempt categorizing on their own) would be most effective. A comparison of traits in figure 3.1 includes criteria from the *Standard Dictionary of Folklore.*

Representative legends to use for modeling:

> *The Ring in the Prairie,* by John Bierhorst
> *Tikki Tikki Tembo,* by Arlene Mosel
> *Star Boy,* by Paul Goble

Representative myths to use for modeling:

> *The Earth is on a Fish's Back,* by Natalie Belting
> *The Summer Maker: An Ojibway Indian Myth,* by Margery Bernstein and Janet Kobrin
> *Raven, Creator of the World,* by Ronald Melzcak (collection also includes legends)
> *Arrow to the Sun,* by Gerald McDermott
> *Sunflight,* by Gerald McDermott

FIGURE 3.1. Comparing myths and legends.

	MYTHS	LEGENDS
TELLER'S BELIEF	Told as fact	Told as fact

SETTING	Remote past
	Gods living on
	    earth
		Historic time
		    & place
		Recognizable world

NATURE OF TALE	Sacred Creation of world Origins of natural events	Sacred or secular Changes in creation Shape changing Heroic deeds
PRINCIPAL CHARACTERS	Deities Supernatural powers	Humans or animals acting like humans

MAKING RELEVANT COMPARISONS

In studying folk literature, the comparing and contrasting of stories develops almost spontaneously. In a sixth grade class, when "Vassilissa the Fair" was being read, children interrupted the story to exclaim, "That's like 'Cinderella'!" Refining this ability can take many avenues:

1. Compare folktales from the same country for use of figurative language typical of that culture, recurring characters, and story structure.
2. Compare folktales from different countries and note the differences in the three elements stated above.
3. Note the presence of universal themes and character traits shared by many cultures.
4. Note universality of humor.

The three sample lessons presented here are designed to develop the students' ability to compare relevant information from multiple sources and recognize agreement or contradiction.

Comparing Legends with Similar Themes

LESSON OBJECTIVE: To compare two legends with similar themes and common motifs and be able to recognize similarities and differences.

MATERIAL: *The Winter Wife* by Anne Crompton; *The Ring in the Prairie* by John Bierhorst

GRADE LEVEL: Third through sixth.

PROCEDURE:

1. Announce that you will read two stories and compare them to see how they are alike and how they are different. *Winter Wife* is an Indian legend from the Abenaki tribe, which lived in the northwest part of the United States, and the *Ring in the Prairie* is from the Shawnee tribe, which lived in the central eastern United States.

2. Read *Winter Wife* using a directed listening-thinking approach, stopping periodically to ask:
   a. What do you think will happen next?
   b. Why do you think so?
   c. (Later in story) Did it happen the way you expected? If not, what changed and why?

3. Read the *Ring in the Prairie* following the same procedure.

4. Direct the pupils to draw a vertical line down the middle of a paper. To the left of the line, they write "Alike" and to the right, "Different." Write the names of the two books at the top of the paper.

5. Teacher-led discussion follows, with the teacher guiding by asking questions related to the elements of a story, such as:
   a. What is the same about the setting, characters, problem, actions, and resolution?
   b. What is different about the setting, characters, problem, actions, and resolution?
      Note: Children are able to respond to similarities more quickly than to differences. When adapting this lesson, with appropriate stories for young children, the teacher must be very sure to elicit similarities first, and then ask probing questions to build recognition of differences.

6. Both books contain artwork worthy of note. Children can compare illustrations with teacher guidance:
   a. Describe the colors each artist uses.
   b. Describe how the lines of the drawings are similar or different.
   c. (If mood has been explained) What kind of a feeling do you get about the mood of the story from each artist?

7. Which were more important, the things that were alike, or the things that were different?

Using the children's response to that question, reiterate the idea that some folktales will be alike or different in message, characters, setting, story action, and resolution of problem.

Comparing Variants of the Same Tale

The fact that the same tale appears in the folk literature of many different countries, with variations that usually result from cultural differences, is intriguing to both the young and the adult reader. Developing the ability to compare these variations can lead to interest in finding out more about the different countries and peoples both geographically and culturally. Currently, the best source of variants with extensive cross-indexing is *The Storyteller's Sourcebook: A Subject, Title, and Motif Index to Folklore Collections for Children* by Margaret Read MacDonald (1982). One can select a favorite tale and find the source of variant tales.

Comparison charts offer a visual means of organizing the similarities and differences children find in stories. Charts can be an individual or group project. The teacher or children can select their own criteria for comparison, such as fairy, animal, legend, or myth characteristics or questions about the content. The chart in figure 3.2 was made by a fifth grader named Dulci who

FIGURE 3.2. Dulci explains her chart comparing Cinderella tales from many countries.

who enjoyed reading as many Cinderella stories as she could find. She chose her own questions. The comparison in the group lesson described below uses the story structure as a basis for comparison.

LESSON OBJECTIVE: To compare the content of three variants of a tale using story structure.

MATERIAL: *The Gingerbread Boy* by Paul Galdone, *The Bun* retold by Marcia Brown, and *The Pancake* retold by Peter Asbjornsen (in Edna Johnson et al., *Anthology of Children's Literature*), for first or second grade level.

PROCEDURE:

1. Read the three variant tales to the whole class.
2. Present poster with the outline of the chart shown in figure 3.3. The elements of the chart are the same as in story maps. If mapping has been taught, the children will be able to respond freely.
3. Divide the class into three groups. Each group completes a chart for one of the stories. The teacher would meet with the groups of younger children. Older children can complete the chart on their own.
4. Compare charts. Encourage discussion of "Why do you think . . . ?" questions concerning the similarities and differences. Curiosity stimulated will lead to more reading and a heightened awareness of the universality of literary expression.

Comparing a Book and a Film

LESSON OBJECTIVE: To compare a film and a book presentation of the same legend, and evaluate the effectiveness of portrayal of character, setting, and similarities or differences in the plot.

MATERIAL: *The Loon's Necklace*, book by William Toye and film by B. F. Sound Films.

GRADE LEVEL: 4th through 8th. Film portrayal may be too frightening for younger children.

Note: The use of symbolism is developed much more extensively in the film than in the book, with the number 4 used in the medicine man's healing orders, in shooting arrows to the sky, and with the dives into the water. The shell necklace had meaning as part of the medicine man's tradition before it became the loon's necklace.

PROCEDURE:

1. Show the film. Note that the film was made before the book.
2. Read the book aloud to the class.

FIGURE 3.3. Comparison chart based on story structure.

BOOK	The Gingerbread Boy by Paul Galdone	The Bun by Marcia Brown	The Pancake by Peter Asbjornsen
SETTING			
Where	In the country	In the country	In the country
When	Long ago	Long ago	Long ago
CHARACTERS	Old Man & Old Woman	Old Man & Old Woman	Goody & Goodman
Who	Gingerbread boy	Bun	7 children—"bairns"
	Cow, Horse, Men	Hare, Wolf, Bear,	Pancake
	threshing wheat,	Fox	Manny-Panny, Ducky-Lucky
	Mowers, Fox		Henny-Penny, Goosey-Poosey
			Cocky-Locky, Gander-Pander
			Piggy-Wiggy
PROBLEM	The gingerbread boy ran away	The bun ran away	The pancake rolled away
ACTION 1	The man & woman run after him but he runs too fast	Bun meets a hare & sings his way out of being caught	The family can't catch him
ACTION 2	Cow can't catch him	Wolf can't catch him	Manny-Panny can't catch him
ACTION 3	Horse can't catch him	Bear can't catch him	Henny-Penny can't catch him
ACTION 4	Men threshing wheat can't catch him	Fox asks him to sing on his nose & then on his tongue	Cocky-Locky can't catch him
ACTION 5	Mowers can't catch him		Ducky-Lucky can't catch him
ACTION 6	Fox gives him a ride across the river		Goosey-Poosey can't catch him
ACTION 7			Gander-Pander can't catch him
ACTION 8			Piggy-Wiggy gives him a ride across the brook
RESOLUTION	The fox eats the gingerbread boy	The fox eats the bun	The pig eats the pancake

3. Guide a discussion developing the following points:
   a. The two demonstrate how differently legends can be interpreted by different storytellers.
   b. Compare the character of the old man as revealed in each medium. How were your feelings about the man drawn out by the author? How were they drawn out in the film?
   c. List the differences between the stories.
        Which story was more exciting?
        Which let you sense what was going to happen next more clearly?
        Which included more detail?
        Compare the illustrations in the book with the film.
4. A natural follow-up activity would be mask-making and dramatic role playing.

MAKING JUDGMENTS

The extent to which the teacher is able to develop this skill will be determined by the developmental level of the child. The reader should understand what the author has said before attempting to pass judgment. Developing this ability helps readers progress beyond making such statements as "I liked it," "It was sad," "It was funny," and provide reasons for their opinions about the stories.

Three lessons are described here. The teaching strategy for each follows the basic four steps explained in previous lessons:

1. State what the teacher intends the reader to discover.
2. Read a story or show film.
3. Discuss during and after reading.
4. Provide for pupil response.

Judgments Based on Clearly Defined Standards

LESSON OBJECTIVE: To make judgments concerning the interpretation of the story.
MATERIAL: "Reflections—Japanese Folktale," Intermediate Film Selection, Encyclopedia Britannica, 1975.

PROCEDURE:
1. View the film.
2. Discuss the film with the group, guiding them toward understanding that the absence of certain information affects the conclusions that are drawn and the judgments that are made.
   a. Why did the story end that way?
   b. If you could enter the story (talk to the characters) what would you do?
   c. Would the characters change their minds (or actions), if you told them what you know?
   d. Their conclusions can be applied to real life and the fact that we often have to make judgments when we do not know all sides of an issue.

Analyzing and Evaluating Conclusions

LESSON OBJECTIVE: To be able to analyze and evaluate conclusions drawn in a story.
MATERIAL: Animal stories are appropriate for introducing this critical reading skill. The behavior of the trickster is clearly stated, and easier to analyze than more complex tales. Select stories from collections such as *Terrapin's Pot of Sense* by Harold Courlander, *Zomo the Rabbit* by Hugo Sturton, *Indian Tales* by Joseph and Edith Raskin, or *One Trick Too Many* by Mirra Ginsburg.
PROCEDURE:
1. Read the story to the class.
2. Discuss two questions:
   a. How does the storyteller present the character so convincingly?
   b. What can you learn about the culture of the people who told this tale?
3. After the children have read animal stories on their own, ask the above questions for them to answer from their independent reading. Vary the mode of response: oral discussion, making a comparison chart, or writing an essay.

Appreciating Illustrated Books

Currently, numerous versions of single folktales are being published with profuse and brilliant artwork. The art of the picture book is valuable not only for enhancing the text, but also for exposing children to a variety of art styles. While working with a number of sixth grade classes, I found that many children tend to pay little attention to the illustrations, but after making comparisons, they become interested in and skilled at comparing and evaluating the artist's contributions to the story.

LESSON OBJECTIVE: To make judgments about the contribution of illustration to understanding, sensing, and appreciating the story.

MATERIAL: See list below for examples of books from specific countries.

PROCEDURE:

1. Discuss your objective for looking at the pictures in several illustrated folktales from one country.
2. Define terms that students will need to know, such as "artist's style." The concept should include the way the artist interprets the story, as shown by choice of medium, color, and the use of line.
3. Ask questions directed toward analyzing the artwork:
   a. What does the picture tell you (content)?
   b. How much of the story can you imagine by looking at the picture? What does the artist use to get you to imagine?
   c. Does the artist's style fit the story? Why or why not?
   d. Why do you think the artist chose that medium for the book?

Comparing different artists' interpretations of folktales from one country helps children recognize that different approaches are valid, and that everyone does not receive the same visual images. The following books are recommended for comparison:

> African
> > *The Third Gift* by Jan Carew, illustrated by Leo and Diane Dillon
> > *Anansi the Spider* retold and illustrated by Gerald McDermott
> > *Who's in Rabbit's House?* by Verna Aardema, illustrated by Leo and Diane Dillon
> > *A Story, A Story* retold and illustrated by Gail Haley
> American Indian
> > *Buffalo Woman* retold and illustrated by Paul Goble
> > *Arrow to the Sun* retold and illustrated by Gerald McDermott
> > *The Winter Wife* by Anne E. Crompton, illustrated by Robert Parker

The Fire Bringer by Margaret Hodges, illustrated by Peter Parnall

A God on Every Mountain Top by Byrd Baylor, illustrated by Carol Brown

Mexican and Central American

The Riddle of the Drum by Verna Aardema, illustrated by Tony Chen

Oté by Pura Belpré, illustrated by Paul Galdone

Greedy Mariani by Dorothy Carter, illustrated by Trina Hyman

The Lady of Guadalupe retold and illustrated by Tomie de Paola

Spirit Child by John Bierhorst, illustrated by Barbara Cooney

Chinese

Liang and the Magic Paintbrush retold and illustrated by Demi

Tikki Tikki Tembo by Arlene Mosel, illustrated by Blair Lent

Six Chinese Brothers retold and illustrated by Chieng Hou-tien

Yeh-shen by Ai-Ling Louie, illustrated by Ed Young

Suho and the White Horse by Yuzo Otsuka, illustrated by Suekichi Akaba

Canadian Indian and Alaskan

Three Stone Woman retold and illustrated by Glo Coalson

The Loon's Necklace by William Toye, illustrated by Elizabeth Cleaver

Proud Maiden, Tungak and the Sun by Mirra Ginsburg, illustrated by Igor Galanin

The Rescue of the Sun and Other Tales from Far North by Edythe W. Newell, illustrated by Frank Altschuler

Russian

Baba Yaga by Ernest Small, illustrated by Blair Lent

Babushka retold and illustrated by Charles Mikolaycak

Anna and the Seven Swans by Maida Silverman, illustrated by David Small

The Fool of the World and the Flying Ship by Arthur Ransome, illustrated by Uri Shulevitz

Mazel and Shlimazel by Isaac Bashevis Singer, illustrated by Margot Zemach

RECOGNIZING THEMES

Along with the themes of the folktales come the moral and ethical values that are inherent in the stories as a part of the culture of the people. The storyteller uses certain concepts, images, and sensuous experiences that bring to life the people, action, and scene in the stories. The readers bring their own beliefs, personalities, past experiences, associations, and mood of the moment to their contemplation of the stories. This produces a unique experience for each reader. The role of the teacher is to foster a relationship between the story and the reader that focuses on the literary work. The teacher cannot ignore the particular bias of the story, or his own ethical bias, but must assist the readers in understanding their own moral values through reading the story. Three lessons are directed toward helping children probe the meaning of stories they read.

Recognizing the Same Theme in Different Stories

LESSON OBJECTIVE: To recognize the same theme developed in different stories from different points of view.

MATERIAL: *The Lazies: Tales of the People of Russia* told by Mirra Ginsburg.

GRADE LEVEL: Fourth through sixth.

PROCEDURE:

1. Describe theme as a message from the author that tells us something about life. The book *The Lazies* is a collection of stories passed down from family to family in Russia to warn people about bad habits.
2. Prereading questions:
   a. What bad habit do you think is the theme of these stories?
   b. How do you think the author will warn you about laziness?
3. Read two stories: "Lazy Shedula" and "The Princess Who Learned to Work." After each story, elicit responses on how the author revealed the theme.
   a. How did the author show you that Shedula was lazy? That the princess was lazy?
   b. Draw attention to what the characters do and say that show the results of laziness.
4. Compare the way the storyteller gives the message in each tale.
   a. How does "The Princess Who Learned to Work" warn against laziness?

b. How is the way this story warns different from the message in "Lazy Shedula?"

c. Can you say in your own words what the theme of each story is?

Recognizing Themes in Fables

A fable is a complex tale. Even though it is short and concise, many young readers cannot understand how the stated moral or proverb relates to the episodes of the story. Through oral sharing of a number of Aesop's fables, the teacher can direct the students to recognize those elements of the story that point to the moral stated.

LESSON OBJECTIVE: To be able to recognize how a fable develops the basis for the stated moral.

MATERIAL: *Aesop's Fables* selected and illustrated by Michael Hague; chart paper.

PROCEDURE:

1. Begin with stating the moral of the familiar fable, "The Hare and the Tortoise."
2. Direct the pupils to listen for actions that lead to the lesson that "slow and steady wins the race."
3. Read the story. Elicit responses that lead to the theme:

   The hare starts out fast.

   The hare stops to take a nap.

   The tortoise starts slowly.

   The tortoise plods without stopping.

   The hare wakes up too late.

   The tortoise gets to the finish line first.
4. State, or have children state, the reasons those statements are important. (The final inference cannot be made without the supporting evidence.)

Recognizing Unstated Themes

Even though the moral is stated, the relationship between the story action and the moral is inferred, not stated. Therefore, oral discussion is necessary to help the readers see how they are making inferences.

LESSON OBJECTIVE: To use the skill gained from finding story elements in fables to discover unstated themes in other stories.

MATERIAL: Select a folktale with a clear but unstated theme, such as *The Third Gift* by Jan Carew, *Mouse Woman and the Mischief Makers* by Christie Harris, *The Blind Boy and the Loon* by Ramona Maher, or *Liang and the Magic Paintbrush* by Demi.

PROCEDURE:

1. Teacher guidance will help develop the questioning attitude that leads to thinking beyond the plot to the message the storyteller wishes to share. State that in reading this story we want to discover the message the story tells about life.
2. Ask questions during and after the reading, such as:
   a. What is the purpose of the character's actions?
   b. What happens in the story that gives you clues as to what the author wants to tell the reader?
   c. Can you find a conversation that gives a clue? How does that help you decide what the message is?

SUMMARY

The objectives of the specific critical reading lessons in this chapter are to classify types and characteristics of folktales, to draw comparisons, to make judgments based on text and artwork, and to recognize themes. The procedures used with these four skills can be adapted for any other aspect of critical reading that you wish to teach. Sixth graders who had scored low in a critical reading test made significant gains after three months of instruction based on these procedures (Bosma, 1981).

Whenever folk literature is used to improve the art and skill of reading, it is important to maintain enjoyment of the stories. The strategies explained in this chapter are intended to advance interest in and appreciation of the literature, rather than provide minute examination of details, which lessens children's interest in reading.

4

Learning to Write
with Folk Literature

The purpose of writing down stories is to pass them and their messages on to a larger audience than could be reached through oral communication. The goal of teaching writing in the elementary classroom is to enhance children's ability to communicate through their own writing. The study of folk literature fosters the reading-writing connection and provides children with successful writing experiences.

This chapter addresses using folk literature as a model of form, theme, and content. Figure 4.1 outlines the elements of models for writing.

FOLKTALE FORM

The predictable structure of the folktale, which assists the reader in understanding the story, also serves to help the writer formulate a story. Many of the nursery tales contain a recurring phrase or rhyme, which the reader can anticipate by the rhythm of the story. In *The Three Little Pigs,* the young listener quickly joins in on "He huffed, and he puffed . . . " and in *Three Billy Goats Gruff* expects to hear "trip, trap" when each billy goat goes over the bridge.

Other stories, such as *The House That Jack Built,* are built on cumulative patterns in which each episode is built upon the previous one with a predictable overlapping structure.

Many fairy tales share beginning phrases such as "Once upon a time," immediately introduce the characters, and tell the story in a direct manner with the ending firmly stated. This matches the child's narrative sense, and can be used to encourage the reluctant writer.

FIGURE 4.1. A web of ways to use folktales as models for writing.

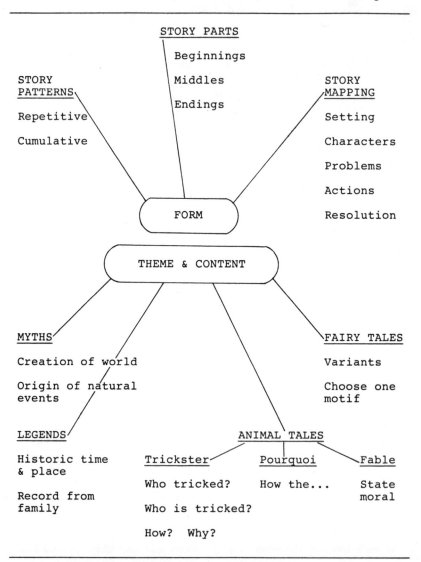

For children at any grade level, prewriting activities provide a helpful way to begin. Prewriting provides the action and participation needed to stimulate creation. Providing story starters is not enough for many writers. They need practice with words and ideas before they feel comfortable writing on their own.

Repetitive Story Patterns

The Great Big Enormous Turnip by Alexei Tolstoy, or a similar book with repetitive phrases, is a good beginning for use in a prewriting activity. First read the story, with the children chanting the repetitive phrase. Then display sentence strips prepared with names or a key word omitted. Elicit original names or words to produce a variant of the story. This can begin as a group activity, and become individual storymaking as soon as the child is ready.

Group story writing helps the reluctant writer. It is easier to provide a word or phrase than to create an entire idea. Confidence builds as the child sees the writing process happening. Listening to other children's ideas stimulates participation. After children listen and respond orally to familiar stories such as *The Three Billy Goats Gruff, The Three Little Pigs,* or *The Gingerbread Boy,* they can create a new story. When the group responds to oral creating, the teacher records the process on chart paper.

LESSON OBJECTIVE: To build a new story using the form of a familiar tale.

MATERIALS: Lesson is based on *The Three Billy Goats Gruff,* as an example. You may choose another story if you prefer.

PROCEDURE:

1. Discuss the components of the story. How many billy goats are there? Where did they go? How did they get there? What is the problem? Fill out a chart like the one below with the children's responses.
2. Plan the main components of the new story in comparison to the story read. Ask for ideas for animals, places to go, how to get there, and the danger along the way. The process chart below was made with first graders.

FOLKTALE	OUR STORY
3 billy goats	3 teddy bears
to the meadow	to the berry patch
across the bridge	through the forest
an ugly troll	a giant who eats bears

trip, trap   thud, thump
Who's going over   Who's going across my
    my bridge?   path?

3. Next, brainstorm a descriptive word chart. What words were used in the folktale that told us about the characters? What words should we use for our story?

FOLKTALE	OUR STORY
Billy goats	*Teddy bears*
youngest	littlest
tiniest	middle-sized
second	great big
bigger	first
third	second
biggest	third
Troll	*Giant*
ugly	wicked
mean	enormous

4. Begin group composing, with the process chart and the word chart taped alongside a fresh piece of chart paper. The teacher records when a consensus is reached about the content. This may take longer than one period. Review the process and word charts if the lesson continues to a second setting to provide the continuity that is needed to create the end product.

How similar the new story and the folktale are will depend on the creative freedom of the group. Some children need to hold on to the familiar structure throughout many experiences, and others are ready to move freely to a new creation. This lesson format can be used with older children having difficulty with writing. Read interesting, simple stories such as *Wiley and the Hairy Man* by Molly Bang or *Strega Nona* by Tomie dePaola.

Cumulative Tales

The same procedure used with the nursery tales can be used with cumulative tales, using charts for planning. The writing lesson should be preceded by the sharing of several books with predictable patterns such as *Henny-Penny, One Fine Day, Bringing the Rain to Kapiti Plain,* and *The Fisherman and His Wife. No Room: An Old Story Retold, Always Room for One More, Hee-Haw,* and *Tikki Tikki Tembo* offer more sophisticated patterns and can be used after the children have enjoyed and recognized the patterns in simpler tales. The following lesson format could be based on any one of the cumulative tales.

LESSON OBJECTIVE: To guide the children in sentence building by adding adjectives or changing verbs. (Begin with selecting one or the other: do not do both in one lesson.)

MATERIAL: *One Fine Day* retold by Nonny Hogrogian; chart paper; figures from the story, traced and cut from tagboard (optional).

PROCEDURE:

1. Reread the story, using the figures to trigger the pupils' memory of story sequence.
2. Note that the storyteller was eager to tell us what would happen next and didn't use many words to describe characters or objects in the story.
3. Select phrases or sentences from the story that contain one adjective or none. Guide the children to add other descriptors like the fox, the cow, or the old woman.
4. After many words have been brainstormed, rewrite the last cumulative sequence, including a descriptive word provided by the children wherever one would fit.
5. When substituting verbs, consider dividing the long sentences into phrases so that the learners can sense the structure:

   Give me your jug / so I can fetch some water / to give the field / to get some grass / to feed the cow . . .

A second grader at Stepping Stones Montessori School in Grand Rapids, Michigan, made these changes:

   A chestnut-colored fox came upon a kind, wonderful miller and asked him, "Oh please, kind miller, give me a little grain to give to the chuckling, big, fat hen to get a hard-boiled white egg."

Using Fairy Tales to Begin the Story

The narrative form of the fairy tale provides a no-nonsense approach that helps the writer put thoughts down in a straightforward manner. This matches the oral story form that children have been using since learning to talk. When children begin to write, many have difficulty beginning or ending a story, or providing coherent action involving their chosen characters. Prewriting lessons, directed towards one of these elements, helps the young writer create.

Using the fairy tale story form does not limit the child to writing fairy tales. This form can be used for any content. The emphasis of prewriting lessons is not on what the child writes, but on how the child expresses the message in an interesting and complete style. Once children are comfortable with a straightforward narrative style, they will be able to depart from it, and provide their own variations.

LESSON OBJECTIVE: To help writers who have difficulty beginning their stories.

MATERIAL: Fairy tales previously read to the class.

PROCEDURE:

1. Tell the group that you are going to think about the way the storytellers begin their stories.
2. Reread just the beginning phrases or first paragraph of fairy tales that were previously read to the class. Also read the beginnings of the same tale told by different authors. For example, "Cinderella" as told by Grimm and Perrault.
3. Ask the children, "Which beginning makes you curious about what is going to happen? Why? Which one tells you the most about the story?"
4. Brainstorm a topic that the class could write about, but do not necessarily plan to create a story. This is a process lesson that will transfer to later writing. At this time, simply use the topics to create several beginnings.
5. Write the brainstormed beginnings on chart paper. Analyze each beginning with the class. Which one would make you want to read on? Why? Which one tells you what to expect in the story?
6. Since this is a process lesson that should transfer to later writing, end the lesson here. Later, when children are ready to write, remind them of this experience and encourage them to think of these models or look at a fairy tale for ideas.

Ending the Story

A lesson on endings can follow a similar format, with a selection of endings from a variety of stories to analyze. Some cultures have distinctive endings for their tales. For example, Norwegian fairy tales often end with "Snip, snap, snout. This tale's told out."

These are some steps you can take to help your students end their tales.

1. Ask children to read aloud the last paragraph or sentence from folktales that you have shared previously.
2. Discuss similarities and differences between examples.
3. Then brainstorm ending phrases and sentences. This process can help the writer avoid simply stopping and writing THE END.

The Middle Section

Improving the middle section of the story requires a series of lessons in which children follow the sequence of the plot and examine how the storyteller develops the characters. The use of the story map helps organize the sequence of the main part of the story if it contains a problem. If the story form is repetitive, help the writer decide how many actions are needed to follow the pattern. For example, in *The Great Big Enormous Turnip,* two people and three animals were called to help. Therefore, the middle of the story needed five episodes before the story could end.

Are the writers having trouble creating authentic characters? Look again at the folktales you have been reading together, and note the actions and conversations of the characters that help you understand their personalities. Generally, folktales contain few descriptions. The prewriting lesson described in the "Cumulative Tales" section can help children use descriptive words.

If the proposed story will present and solve a problem, a story map is a practical planning device. The act of mapping helps the children think through their story ideas and provides an outline from which they can create. This is particularly helpful when time limits make it impossible to finish the story in one sitting. Present the writers with the form shown in figure 2.1 (page 14) or a variation that would fit their proposed story structure. Then list the actions that lead to the solution. Teachers who have used this procedure report that it has been a major factor in improving the quality of the writing of their pupils.

FOLKTALE THEME AND CONTENT

Just as prewriting activities help writers understand story structure, informal writing helps writers capture ideas from the themes and content of the stories they hear. Informal writing is recorded in a journal or notebook and kept by the child, rather than evaluated or edited by the teacher.

After the teacher reads a story aloud, many children are eager to make a remark about the story—about personal experiences, the artwork, some words that caught their fancy, or a reaction to the character, action, or ending of the story. There is never time to listen to everyone. Following discussion, informal writing presents an opportunity to make the writing a continuation of the thinking process stimulated by the oral interchange. If the teacher develops the habit of giving a few moments for the children to write these thoughts down, they become familiar with writing as a communication process, and also recognize that their thoughts are important and worthwhile to record. These recorded thoughts can become the stimulus for a poem or topic for a story.

Myths

Origins are intriguing to children. Even the child who has difficulty recognizing and verbalizing imaginative thoughts can spark a "what if" stance and provide fanciful explanations for how things came to be. What if there were no stories in the world?

LESSON OBJECTIVE: To create a myth.
MATERIAL: *A Story, a Story* by Gail Haley; other myths (see step 6, below).
PROCEDURE:
1. Read Gail Haley's version of "A Story, a Story," which gives an African explanation for how stories were hidden from humans.
2. Lead children in brainstorming other ideas for hiding, then releasing, stories.
3. Choose a country, perhaps one that you are currently studying in social studies.
4. As a group, list descriptive words that would help express ideas.
5. Ask children to select from the brainstormed lists, and write their own explanations of how stories entered the world in that particular country.
6. Discuss other mythical topics. *The Summer Maker* or *The First Morning* by Margery Bernstein and Janet Kobrin, *How Summer Came to Canada* by William Toye, and *Daughters of the Earth* by Gerald McDermott all explain the origin of seasons.
7. Engage the students in brainstorming other beginnings for seasons.
8. Discuss which people would be the audience for the story.
9. Encourage the children to select their own topics and write an explanation for their chosen audience.

The brainstorming process is important for generating ideas. The more stories that the students hear, the better they will become at producing their own writing. The sense of story, which is refined through hearing literary models, becomes the spring from which ideas flow.

After a lesson based on the above procedure, a fourth grader at Rehoboth Christian School, Rehoboth, New Mexico, wrote the following myth:

> A long time ago the Sun, Moon, and Stars all shone during the day. The people hated it because the farmers' crops withered, the windows melted from the hot sun, and all of the plants dried up. There was no water for the river, so the people couldn't have any water to drink, and the babies could not get to sleep.
>
> So then the Sun, Moon, and Stars quarreled about who would shine during the night and who would shine during the day.
> Finally the Sun beat down on the Moon and Stars and said, "If you don't let me shine during the day, I will beat on you so bad that you will never be able to shine again!" So the Moon and Stars said they would shine during the night, and the Sun quit beating on them. And so the Sun shone during the day and the Moon and Stars shone at night.
>
> The people were very happy! They had lots of rain, the crops grew good, the windows were replaced, and the babies could finally get to sleep.
>
> *Jeff Boyd*

Legends

The recording of oral folklore is not limited to the professional storyteller. Groups who have moved to America have produced folklore collections that reveal much about their culture. For example, the Cambodian people who settled in the southside of Minneapolis told their stories during a language project at Our Saviour Lutheran Church. The stories were collected and typed under the direction of Charles Numrich of Theatre Unlimited.

Byrd Baylor, author of stories about the southwest, collected legends from Arizona Indian children and wrote them exactly as the children remembered hearing them from their parents and grandparents. The resulting book, *And It Is Still That Way,* is discussed in chapter seven.

Recording family legends can be an exciting and challenging class project. Preparation would include discussing procedures for talking to family members and recording the interviews. Appropriate questions should be formulated in class for the children to take to the person who may know the stories. If possible, the child can collect the information on a tape recorder, and then transcribe the tape. If no tape recorder is available, the child should write down everything the adult says. Having listened to many folktales, the child will be able to include the literary conventions of the folktale when rewriting the information.

Nancy DeVries, reading teacher at Kennedy Mid School, Gallup, New Mexico, collected folk anecdotes from a summer remedial reading class. The Indian and Hispanic children were reading *Tiger Eyes* by Judy Blume, and encountered the phrase, "when the lizards run." They had heard their mothers and grandmothers use that saying frequently. The group decided to ask their families what the saying meant, and write down what they were told. The children wrote and edited their stories on computers using the wordprocessing program Bank Street Writer. They were so excited about their writing that on the last day of school they chose to finish copying their stories, instead of having a party. The explanations they gave varied greatly. Note that some have written the anecdote exactly as reported and others have expanded it into a story.

> In the Navajo way, first my Grandpa told me every spring the lizards run because, they have been under the ground for so long. When winter comes they go underground for the winter. After the winter they come out of the ground. Then they run around in the summer.
>
> *Vernon Yazzie*

> When the lizards run is because the ancestors are coming back to live in the spring. The ancestors used to race lizards for money a long time ago, to see who runs the fastest. . . . Some ancestors used to sell them to the white men.
>
> *Ross*

> When the lizards run it is time for spring. It is time for joy and laughter and spring showers. Spring showers wash down and melt snow so lizards could run around freely. I like it when the lizards run because I chase them all over the place. It is fun . . . they cheer you up and make you laugh when you are sad or unhappy.
>
> *Shawn*

FIGURE 4.2. Sixth graders at Gallup, New Mexico, rewrite their legends on computers using a wordprocessing program.

I'll hear the birds singing. I'll smell the lilac bushes, and I'll watch the iris bloom. *Cuando los lagartijos corren* . . . life is a good adventure in the spring. Lizards wake us up to get us ready for the fun of summer.

Miguel

Nancy DeVries reported:

Remedial students, "sentenced" to summer school, developed sophisticated skills in creating and revising during the writing process, and were able, many for the first time, to have a real pride of accomplishment in their work. An additional value that developed from using folk literature was a sharing of cultural stories and heritages, and with this sharing a mutual respect emerged, rather than the previous aloof distrust prevalent between the different Indian tribes and Spanish or Anglo ethnic groups. (Personal communication, Sept. 1985)

At Christmas time, Mrs. DeVries's class wrote family folktales to give as gifts for younger brothers, sisters, or cousins. The tales were read or performed in class. One Indian girl discovered that some of her ancestors were from the Acoma tribe. She retold and illustrated the story of Young Hunter told to her by her Acoma grandmother.

YOUNG HUNTER

This is a story of the Acoma Indians. It is about a boy named Young Hunter who had a big head and how he saved a girl.

Long ago there lived a boy named Young Hunter. He was a very shy boy because he had such a big ugly head. One day the Chief called all the boys together for a meeting. Young Hunter joined the meeting. The Chief was talking about a girl named Pink Flower who had been taken away by the Giant who lived sixty miles away. He told them whoever saved her could marry her or a girl called Turquoise Girl. So he packed his clothes and said good-bye to his grandmother and left. He met a rain god on the way and kept him for protection. They got to a mesa and the rain god said, "I have to leave you here. Go on. Here are some herbs. Chew them as you walk. Spit them out when you see danger."

So he went on. Then he heard the god's voice say, "Don't kill the Giant!"

The next day he saw the girl. He whispered, "Come, we must go before the giant wakes up!"

So he spit out some of the herbs and they flew to where he had left the rain god and all of a sudden he heard the giant scream and die.

The next day he returned to the village with Pink Flower. Everybody cheered. Turquoise Girl came to help the Grandmother. She was taken into a room filled with soft buckskin and strings of turquoise beads. She was taken into a room all bare except for a mask. The mask of a young hunter. The grandmother said, "Young Hunter has passed his test!" She called Young Hunter into the room and a handsome man whom she had never seen before stepped into the room. On the day the marriage was celebrated Turquoise Girl made loaves of bread and did household tasks for the man she loved. (Retold by Kimberlee Evans, part Acoma Indian, J. F. Kennedy Mid School, Gallup, New Mexico).

FIGURE 4.3. Kimberlee shows the class the setting for her Acoma legend.

Animal Tales

Animal tales provide an entertaining model for writing. Trickster stories are easier for children to write than fables because they are structured and direct.

LESSON OBJECTIVE:　To write a trickster tale.

MATERIAL:　Such trickster tales as *One Trick Too Many* by Mirra Ginsburg, *Complete Tales of Uncle Remus* (Br'er Rabbit) by Joel Harris, *Badger, the Mischief Maker* by Kay Hill, *Coyote the Trickster* by Gail Robinson and David Hill, and *The Dancing Granny* by Ashley Bryan.

PROCEDURE:

1. Share the tales.
2. As a prewriting activity, chart the stories using a form such as one shown in figure 4.4.
3. Discuss the role of the trickster as sometimes a hero, sometimes a naughty tricker.

4. When children are ready to write their trickster tales, they should first outline or put in charts the needed elements in the story. Then they can decide whether their animal will be a hero or a naughty tricker.
5. Consider creating a class trickster. Each pupil could write an adventure for the chosen animal.

Pourquoi animal tales are usually titled "Why the [name of animal] has [a particular feature]." These are similar to legends, but are exaggerated and humorous because they were not believed, but created for entertainment. A good model for introducing writing of pourquoi stories is the *Just So Stories* of Rudyard Kipling. His created stories can be compared with traditional tales such as *Cherokee Animal Tales* by George Scheer, *Indian Tales* by Raskin, *The Long-tailed Bear* by Natalie Belting, and *Why Mosquitoes Buzz in People's Ears* by Verna Aardema. Here is a good opportunity to discuss the difference between traditional stories and those originating from a known author. Direct pupils to check how the author is identified. Do they find the words *retold by, translated, compiled,* or similar expressions? Are there notes concerning the origins of the stories? If not, the stories are modern, invented tales, such as the ones children write. Teaching the writing of pourquoi stories calls for a procedure similar to that used for teaching the writing of myths.

1. Read models from both traditional and original stories.
2. Brainstorm ideas for various animals and features.
3. Discuss the possibilities and the limitations of form: one main character animal, one feature of the animal explained in the story. Other animals can be supporting characters.
4. Use a chart, such as shown with the trickster stories, or a story map to plan the elements of the story.

Arnold Lobel's original *Fables* provides an excellent model for children who are writing fables. Comparing modern fables with versions of Aesop's and Jataka fables will ease the transition from reading the stories to writing them. Since composing a fable requires a relatively high level of thinking ability, this writing experience will be more productive above the third grade level. After reading and discussing many fables, select one of two variant strategies:

1a. Make a list of morals or proverbs, such as "Don't count your chickens before they hatch." Each child can select one moral or proverb as the theme for an original fable.

FIGURE **4.4.** Chart of trickster tales.

NAME OF STORY	WHO TRICKED?	WHO WAS TRICKED?	TRICK	RESULT

1b. Or, make a list of human faults in a brainstorming session. Practice making an original proverb that cautions against that fault. Write the story that provides an explanation, ending with a moral.
2. Using either 1a or 1b, elicit from the children possible characters and adjectives to describe them.

Fairy Tales

A comparison of modern fairy tales, such as Jane Yolen's *A Girl Who Cried Real Flowers* or Oscar Wilde's *The Selfish Giant* and the traditional fairy tale demonstrates to children that writing fairy tales is a legitimate use of story form. The comparison will also reveal that the modern fairy tale can be written more simply than the traditional tale, which usually interweaves many motifs.

The idea of selecting one motif as the topic of an original fairy tale helps develop the creative flow of ideas for the child writer.

LESSON OBJECTIVE: To write a fairy tale.
MATERIAL: A modern fairy tale such as Wilde's *The Selfish Giant.*
PROCEDURE:
1. Tell the children that the modern tale is original, rather than retold or written down from oral tradition. Review the characteristics of a fairy tale presented in chapter one.
2. Direct writers to choose one motif, such as, three wishes, a seemingly impossible task, or a supernatural object as a source of magic, to give the writer courage to attempt this more complicated story form. A brainstorming session would be helpful in making this choice.

3. After selecting the motif, decide on characters and setting for the story.
4. Encourage independent writing, and the sharing of stories with partners for help in preparing a final draft.

Guard against requiring the children to restage traditional tales into modern day settings. These attempts are usually not successful below the age of twelve because time and space relationships are difficult for young children to manipulate.

Students may write variants of familiar tales such as "Cinderella," 'Snow White," or "Hansel and Gretel." To have them do this:

1. Begin by reading several different versions of the stories.
2. Discuss the similarities and differences.
3. The children can either create their own version, or invent new characters and episodes following the story line of the modeled fairy tale.

Some children may elect to change the setting from the olden days to modern times, and such a choice would indicate that those children had developed a flexible sense of time and space.

SUMMARY

In this chapter, writing is presented as an extension of oral language, with writing activities preceded by literature sharing. Basing lessons on the predictable folktale story form found in nursery stories, cumulative tales, and fairy tales helps the child write with confidence. The examples given in this chapter can be adjusted to any grade level, using other titles described in chapter seven, or similar tales available in local libraries.

Informal writing can become a natural response to listening to and discussing literature. After providing for informal writing time, teachers can work with ideas recorded by the children in informal writing by turning once again to folk literature for models to improve the writers' craft. Lessons using myths, legends, animal tales, and fairy tales provide opportunities for young writers to grow in their writing performance.

5

Creative Activities
with Folk Literature

The imaginative quality of folk literature clamors for creative response. Once the readers understand and appreciate the stories, they are able to participate in a variety of creative activities, which in turn enhance reading. In this chapter are suggestions for relating folktales with specific creative encounters. These ideas are presented with the assumption that creative drama, music, and art are already part of the school curriculum. Folktales can be the content of processes already practiced and enjoyed in the classrooms.

IMPROVISING, PANTOMIMING, DRAMATIZING

After the introductions to fairy tales, animal stories, legends, and myths, children can share the stories they have read individually or in small groups by using creative movement. Expressive body movements reveal ideas and feelings that children receive from the story.

While drawing comparisons between two or more variants of tales, the similiarities or differences can be shown by action. Dramatizing *The Gingerbread Boy* and *The Pancake* is not only an enjoyable activity, but demonstrates to the teacher that the children have understood the differences.

Tomie dePaola's art and writing style make his versions of folk stories natural selections for play-acting. His illustrations are drawn from the perspective of an audience viewing a performance. *Strega Nona, Lady of Guadalupe,* or *The Clown of God* provide models for stage props and costumes for in-class performances.

A performance by a professional drama troupe or a nearby college group can be a catalyst for freeing children to participate in creative drama.

FIGURE 5.1
A visiting drama troupe.

Since fables generally have two or three main characters, pupils can develop a partner or team pantomime of the story, with little or no teacher direction. After the children have practiced, the rest of the class becomes the audience. If a narrator for each team states the moral of the fable, the audience will be able to follow the action of the pantomime and interpret the presentation. The use of simple masks enhances the fable presentation.

For ideas on implementing dramatic activities, see *It's Your Move* by Gloria Blatt and Jean Cunningham, *Improvisation Handbook* by Sam Elkind, and *Informal Drama in the Elementary Language Arts Program* by John Stewig.

MASK MAKING

Children become less inhibited doing pantomime and improvisations when using masks. The mask does not hide the child, but rather releases and reveals the child's ability to forget himself and enter into the character.

The making of the mask can be simple: cut card stock or tagboard into oval forms, with eyes and nose cut out, and yarn attached to tie around the child's head. A few simple felt-tip lines can designate eyebrows, mouth, or forehead furrows. More complex masks may be inspired by consulting *Masks, Face Coverings, and Headgear* by Norman Laliberte and A. Mogelon.

A beginning session in which the teacher leads the pupils in expressing themselves through head, neck, arm, torso, and leg movements can free them to attempt story actions. Then give the children free rein in expressing the story character's actions.

The role of masks in folklore is an interesting topic for individuals who are fascinated by *The Loon's Necklace* by William Toye, *Who's in Rabbit's House* by Verna Aardema, or other Indian and African tales. Masks play a significant role in Indian and African folklore.

Leo and Diane Dillon's illustrations of *Who's in Rabbit's House* depict the story as being performed by masked players. The model of that format can help the pupils develop their own ideas for dramatization.

STORYTELLING

The oral tradition of folk literature should be perpetuated by young and old alike. Many children are fascinated by the drama of storytelling, and are willing to spend the time needed to practice the tales. Children can be encouraged to tell the tales to class groups, the whole class, and perhaps other classes in the school. Telling the tales requires the ability to enunciate clearly and read expressively, using effective intonation, pitch, and stress to convey the message. See chapter six for a description of the process that a teacher used with his class.

Many communities have storytelling groups. A local storyteller invited to entertain the class provides an enjoyable model for the children. A visiting storyteller may be willing to answer questions and give valuable tips for preparation of the storytelling experience.

Three valuable sources for techniques are *Handbook for Storytellers* by Carolyn Feller Bauer, *Twenty Tellable Tales* by Margaret MacDonald, and *Storyteller* by Ramon Ross.

MUSIC AND DANCE

Finding appropriate music to accompany storytelling becomes a challenging activity for the children after they understand the mood that the author and illustrator are attempting to convey. Individuals can practice storytelling and set stories to music on cassette tapes to be shared with classmates. The prepared cassettes provide a classroom library for background music that can be used with storytelling, creative drama, and dance responses to literature.

Interpretive dance offers an expressive extension of folk literature. Begin by using excerpts from popular ballets and operettas that are musical renditions of folktales such as *The Sorcerer's Apprentice* or *Sleeping Beauty* (see Riordan, 1984). Encourage the children to move with the music, allowing the music to dictate their movements. The difference between dance and improvisation is that in dance one allows the music to dictate the movements. If the child takes the cues from the music, expressive dance becomes an individual interpretation of the story. Sources for teaching dance include *Children Discover Music and Dance* by Emma Sheehy, *On the Count of One* by Elizabeth Sherbon, and *Action, Gestures, and Bodily Attitudes* by Carolyn Deitering. Deitering's book deals specifically with the liturgical form of dance.

READER'S THEATER

Reader's theater provides creative oral reading within the classroom through two or more oral interpreters bringing a literature experience to an audience.

Certain conventions are generally attended to by the participants:

1. The narrator and readers are seated in a group in front of the audience. High stools make them more visible and provide a distinctive place for the performance.
2. Simple props may be used, but there is no use of scenery or costume that takes the attention away from the oral interpretation.
3. The reader uses the voice to evoke mental images of characters and scenes.
4. The narrator speaks directly to the audience and does not interact with the other readers.
5. Each reader carries the script because the emphasis is on reading, not acting or memorization.
6. An effort is made to develop a personal relationship between the audience and the reader, with an emphasis on the sounds of the language.

Emphasis in classroom reader's theater is on using the voice to produce mental images of characters and scenes. Practicing with partners helps free the reader to develop dramatic expression.

Verna Aardema's books are especially adaptable for reader's theater because of the quantity of dialogue and repetitive ideophones. Russian stories in *The Firebird* by Boris Zvorykin and the Indian tale *The Third Gift* by Jan Carew are fascinating for reader's theater production.

Reader's Theatre: Story Dramatization in the Classroom by Shirlee Sloyer is a useful source of information for the teacher.

PUPPETS

The sharply drawn characters of fairy tales and animal tales make wonderful puppets. From the simplest paper bag puppet to the most elaborate papier-mâché model, storybook characters can be easily identified by accentuating particular features. Hand, rod, or shadow puppets of princes, princesses, and witches can fit any favorite fairy tale. Simple silhouette figures can be jointed with metal fasteners, moved with attached, thin sticks, and projected with an overhead projector. See *Play with Light and Shadow* by Herta Schonewolf (1968). Head puppets of tricksters like Anansi, Br'er Rabbit, Coyote, or Fox can be kept in the classroom for spontaneous dramatic plays of animal tales.

If the children understand the story well, they will be able to provide conversation for their puppets, select background music to set the stage, and develop the story in groups with a minimum of teacher guidance.

For puppet construction and stage ideas see *The Theatre Student and Puppetry—The Ultimate Disguise* by George Latshaw (1978). For learning hand puppet expression, consult *Making Puppets Come Alive* by Carol and Engler Fijan (1973).

VISUAL ART

The art in folk literature provides excellent models for children's artistic exploration. The teacher can provide materials for experimenting with collage, cutting, printing, watercolor, and tempera painting. Read unillustrated stories from collections such as the Courlander tales of Africa, Finger's tales of South America, and Harris's tales of Indian totems. The children can illustrate, choosing media and colors that fit the mood of the story.

FIGURE 5.2. Matt illustrated his revised version of *One Fine Day*.

Story sharing can take the form of book jackets, posters, billboards, and murals designed by the readers. Sequential pictures of the story line can be fastened together to make a simulated movie or television production. Displays of the art work spread the enthusiasm for stories. Books recommended by peers are quickly chosen by another child.

For instructions for using various media, consult Laura Chapman's series, *Discover Art* (1984). *Paper Sculpture* by Pauline Johnson illustrates simple techniques for making such creations as dioramas, murals, and paper costumes.

VISUAL IMAGERY

Some children are not aware that they see pictures in their mind. Building this awareness helps the children relate new ideas with concepts already in their experience. Talking about visual images helps children who are better at imagery than at verbal communcation to express their ideas.

The Formation of the Earth

FIGURE **5.3**
Amy Payne designed a
book cover for her
original myth.

Since visual imagery is not commonly described as a creative activity, a specific lesson is described here for developing the reader's ability to picture ideas in response to literature.

LESSON OBJECTIVE: To develop awareness that words can create a picture in your mind.

MATERIAL: *The Fisherman and His Wife* translated by Randell Jarrell, or any folktale using vivid descriptions or depicting vivid actions.

PROCEDURE:

1. Explain to the children that storytellers use words to create pictures. Try an experiment to show that many words create pictures in our minds. Ask the children to think about what they see when you say a word. Use words that you know are in their experience (e.g., baby, man, lady). Ask for a description of what they see.

2. Suggest that while listening to this story, they pay attention to the kinds of pictures they see in their minds.
3. After the reading, ask for responses, based on the general pictures they received.
4. Focus on certain expressions or statements, such as:

> . . . and when he came to the sea, the water was all violet and dark blue and gray and not so green and yellow any more, but it was still calm. (p. 7)
>
> The sea was all black and thick, and began to boil up from underneath so that it threw up bubbles, and a whirlwind passed over it. (p. 12)
>
> . . . and outside a storm was raging. (p. 23)

5. Ask as many of the following questions as you sense are appropriate for your group:
    a. Describe the most important thing in your mind picture.
    b. Describe the background of your mind picture (be sure to include color).
    c. What is light in the picture? What is dark?
    d. What is moving? What is still?

TASTE, TOUCH, SMELL

LESSON OBJECTIVE: To recognize that words can provoke appeal to taste, touch, and smells.

MATERIALS: A favorite folktale, such as *Mazel and Shlimazel* retold by Isaac Bashevis Singer; chart paper.

PROCEDURE:

1. Have children list words that make them want to taste, touch, or smell something.
2. Select a book that you have read before, so that upon second reading the listeners can concentrate on their feelings.
3. Brainstorm words and phrases for the chart. Ask children to explain why they have chosen those words.

For a reinforcing activity, post a large wall chart. From independent reading, children can write words on the chart. Include book title and page number.

THE SOUND OF LANGUAGE

LESSON OBJECTIVE: To delight in the sound of words.

MATERIAL: An alliterative tale, such as *Bringing the Rain to Kapiti Plain* retold by Verna Aardema or *One Fine Day* by Nonny Hogrogian.

PROCEDURE:

1. Read the story.
2. Encourage children to chant the refrains.
3. Repeat and enjoy as often as you can.

This experience will help children become more word conscious and extend their use of story structure by developing a sense of the rhyme and rhythm of language.

EXPLORING LANGUAGE

The history of the English language can be a captivating study if children are introduced to it with enthusiasm. The egocentric nature of children leads them to believe that language originated in their native tongue, which always existed. Discovering words that originated from folk literature can help children establish a more accurate historic understanding of language.

Not all children are intrigued by word origins, so some need an enthusiastic teacher to encourage them to learn about this subject as an independent challenge. Once children have become interested in word study through exploration of vocabulary in myths and legends, that interest may carry over into other areas.

Mythology offers a good beginning for word study because so many words in every European language derive from Greek and Roman mythology. After Christianity spread throughout the world, educated persons no longer believed the Greek myths, but they continued to read the great literature that was filled with mythological figures and exploits. Words derived from myths were introduced in various languages when new words were coined. Many of those words are recognizable in the English language of today by their prefix or root.

Scientists drew on mythological terminology to name new animals, plants, chemical, or phenomenal discoveries. The Latin or Greek term gave a universality to the new name that made it understandable across many languages. A valuable source of information for discovering the role of myths in the history of language is *Words from the Myths* by Isaac Asimov.

Independent discovery of word origins can proceed from word to story, or from story to word. Both strategies are demonstrated here.

LESSON OBJECTIVE: To discover word origins.
MATERIAL: Bulletin board; color-coded cards.
PROCEDURE:

FROM WORD TO STORY

1. Encourage children by example and discussion to search out word sources.
2. Post an attractive bulletin board on the classroom wall or in a learning center and invite individual participation (See figure 5.4).
3. Specialized lists can be used, such as science words: Arctic Ocean, atlas, brontosaurus, fauna, flora, helium, planet, plutonium, solar, territory, and uranium; or phrases: Achilles' heel, by Jove, Midas touch, work like a Trojan.

FROM STORY TO WORD

1. Tell the children that when they come to a word in a myth or legend that they have heard somewhere else with another meaning, they should look it up in the dictionary. They should check to see if the origin of the word is given.
2. Prepare color-coded cards for the children to use in posting their findings on the bulletin board. They should put the name of the story where the word was found on a card of one color, the word itself on a card of a second color, and its modern meaning on a card of a third color. These cards should be lined up in columns under appropriate headings (Story, Word, Modern Meaning).

SUMMARY

Creative response to folk literature can take many forms: creative drama, mask making, storytelling, music, reader's theater, puppetry, the visual arts, and language exploration. Specific teaching suggestions are given for visual imagery and language exploration. For the other creative responses, the information in this book is limited to the relationship between folk

```
                 WHAT'S THE CONNECTION?

Find out                              Words We Use
1. Where did that word come from?       cosmos
2. What special meaning                 chaos
   of the first word                    echo
   led to making the                    extra-
   new word?                              terrestrial
3. If possible, name a myth or          giant
   legend from folk literature          hero
   that uses the word                   hygiene
   in its original form.                ocean
                                        siren
                                        zephyr
```

```
On this part of the board the children will write
the findings from researching the word, answering
the questions above.

Sources children could use:
   Words from Myths
   Webster's New World Dictionary, or
   another classroom dictionary
```

FIGURE 5.4. Discovering word origins: A model for a bulletin board display.

literature and the activity. Sources are suggested for information pertinent to implementing the activities.

Each activity suggested is, by itself, worthy of merit. In addition, the extent to which the children respond through the activity gives the teacher an indication of how completely the children have understood the characters, story line, and theme of the literature they have read. Interpretation for creative response requires critical thinking about the reading.

6

A Fifth-Sixth Grade Class Uses Folk Literature

This chapter is an account of an actual classroom use of folk literature in a reading and writing program. The class is a combined fifth and sixth grade in Beckwith Public School, Grand Rapids, Michigan. The teacher is John Booy.

TALES AND TOTEM POLES

Jill, Katie, and Kathi carried their brightly decorated five-foot totem down the hall from their classroom to the third grade class. The third graders were sitting on the floor, eagerly awaiting the visit, for the large totems had been very visible in the art room. The girls placed the totem in front of the class, and sat cross-legged next to it. They proceeded to tell their original, well-rehearsed stories, following an Indian tradition. Jill began:

> The first story in this series starts at the top of the family totem pole with Gomokish and his tale of the unicorn. He is the great-grandfather of the totem.
>
> Next comes Naway, the grandfather of the totem, and his exciting legend of the bear and the salmon.
>
> The father of the boy who carved this pole, Iracian, has a wonderful story of himself and the beautiful pelican.
>
> The carver of the totem pole symbolizes the earth in his section for he learned the importance of respect for nature.

FIGURE 6.1
Jill, Katie, and Kathi are ready to follow the Indian storytelling tradition with a visit to the third grade.

Kathi told her story:

HOW THE RAINBOW AFFECTED UNICORNS
WITH THE HELP OF GOMOKISH

One beautiful sunny day in the 1600s, my tribe the Shoshone were all going about our own business, when an old Unicorn, I'd say has been living for at least 15 years, came trotting onto our land looking so much in pain.

Then I, Gomokish, noticed his leg. It was bleeding and he was limping on it. I ran over to him and picked the Unicorn up, gently, and took him to the river to clean the cut out.

"Oh, you poor thing, I will help you." I remember saying. "I will help you."

The Unicorn sort of looked up at me, in a way knowing that I would. I walked from there to the forest trying to find the right leaf to help him. A tree that had a soft, but not brittle leaf that would wrap around its leg to protect the bruise. I know that there should be a tree for him, because Oregon has tons of trees.

When I found one I carefully wrapped the leaf around the Unicorn's cut and took him to my home.

Each day the Unicorn was getting better. I would help it walk and I knew by the way he cooperated with me he very much appreciated it.

When the day came to let the Unicorn go, it was very hard on me. "Little fellow, it's time for you to go."

That's all I said, then I turned around and left, wondering if the Unicorn was going to be happy or not.

A few days after the Unicorn left Oregon, he was trotting happily in the woods, catching some of the last few raindrops, on his pure white fur shaded with brown.

The Unicorn came upon a rainbow while he was walking, and remembering how poor he was, started to climb it, wanting to reach the end for the pot of gold. Once he was in the middle, the Unicorn stopped to take a look around to see the Earth.

The Unicorn turned on the rainbow, trying to get a good look, but he slipped, because of his slippery hooves, and tumbled down the rainbow to where he first started from.

He started to climb it again, but whenever he reached the middle and stopped to take a look around, he would end up where he started from.

The Unicorn knew that if he would just not stop in the middle then he would make it to the end, but he could not bear not stopping to take a look.

When he finally stopped trying to climb the rainbow, and went home, he noticed that the colors of the rainbow had rubbed off on him, so he went to the river to wash off.

When he was done and went back to his home he still had the colors on his horn, so he went back to wash it off, but the colors wouldn't rub off. He scrubbed and scrubbed but nothing would come off.

The Unicorn was one of the oldest ones living, and because of what happened to him all the other Unicorns received the colors of the rainbow on their horns too.

The Unicorn went back to Oregon to see me, Gomokish. I saw him coming, and knew him because of the rainbow on his horn. We both know it was happy and peaceful sign.

Jill told her story, which concerned the middle section of the totem pole:

HOW THE SALMON CAME TO THE WILLAMETTE RIVER

At one time the Shoshone tribe was happy. They lived in a beautiful place with plenty of food and led good lives.

Then something changed. The people became greedy and selfish and soon food became scarce.

The people grew too lazy to hunt so they took the easy task of fishing.

Soon all the big red fish called salmon were gone and there was not a fish left in the stream.

The people began to starve and many died.

A boy called Naway saw the grief of his tribe, but he was happy.

For long ago his parents died and his tribe made him an outcast. He went to live in the forest with a kind old bear he called Nicka.

She provided his food and shelter and the love his mother would have given him.

He knew the people had caused this trouble.

When he returned home that night he said to Nicka, "I must find a way to help my people even though it is they that have brought this upon themselves."

"Yes, my son, I have taught you many powerful secrets. I am sure you'll know which one is best," the old bear replied.

For three days Naway worked on a clay fish. When it was finished he painted it red and it looked like a salmon.

Nicka saw it and chanted her medicine song and told Naway to fetch some water in one of the deerskin bags.

When he returned, his mother, Nicka, put the "fish" in the water and it became alive.

Together they brought it to the stream and let it go.

As the fish dove into the water its number kept multiplying until nearly one hundred fish were in the water.

Naway was proud of his mother for this was the greatest magic the old bear had ever peformed.

Nicka told the boy that he must preach to his people and tell them about the fish and that they must respect the land.

She added, "I will come and kill the village if my laws are not obeyed."

Naway turned and started toward his village. The people were surprised to see him, but listened to his story.

Naway began, "My people, you have taken all the red fish out of the river and now you are dying."

"My mother, Nicka, the great bear and I have given you more fish for your river. Those fish belong to all, nature and our people.

"You must never do this again, it has hurt you and the animals.

"If you turn lazy and disrespectful ever again the red ones will leave your streams never to return.

"But more deathly to you, my peaceful Nicka will come here and kill you all for disobeying her laws!"

The people gazed in horror but praised Naway for returning their fish.

From then on the Shoshone have always held the fish in great honor.

The bear was made sacred and Naway was made chief of the tribe.

The salmon have stayed in the Willamette River and still today the Indians dance the fish dance in honor of the salmon.

Katie pointed to the bottom picture on the totem as she began her storytelling:

THE PELICAN GOD

Long ago there was a tribe called the Shoshones.

Every morning the men of the tribe would leave their home and go to a nearby river to catch some fish.

When they came back the women of the tribe would have a fire ready to cook the large amounts of fish the men had caught.

One morning the men started down toward the river as usual. When they got there they sat and sat with their fishing sticks moving ever slightly by the fall breeze. All day long they sat but no catch.

"There is no fish in this river. Today we come home with nothing," said a tribe member named Iracian.

"Yes, we will starve," said Rackson.

The men started home with empty sacks.

That night everyone was showered over grief. The fires set off a soft glow just enough so you could see the weary faces among the circle. There were streaks of tears across the cheeks of the tribe members.

The fear of starvation swelled up into everyone. The days that passed were the hardest of all.

Still, the men went to the river in the morning then returned when darkness fell. Every night was the same, no fish.

People began to get very hungry, some died and some remained ill.

One night as the Shoshones gathered around the fire, Iracian spoke:

"I know we are all hungry. The fish must've left us, without telling us why. We must have a dance for food tomorrow night or else we will perish. It has to be big and meaningful, if that doesn't work we are hopeless."

The next night a fire crackled in the middle of the circle. Many men were dressed in bright earthly colors.

They danced to the beat of the drums, while the rest of the tribe sang Indian songs.

Soon it ended.

"Now we must wait, we must sleep," Iracian said tiredly.

More days passed and still no sight of food. While the men were out at the river the women scavenged around looking for plants to eat. When they did find some, they were very small, and could not be shared among the whole Shoshone group.

"I see we are all dying of starvation, so I plan to go on a journey in quest of the Pelican God. Surely he will give us food and send the fish back. Then we can live healthy again," said the only brave soul, Iracian.

The next day Iracian set out on his journey.

It was spring so he had no fear of storms. But on the second day a storm came about. Iracian quickly wrapped himself up in his bear furs. His braided black hair blew wildly in the wind. His bare feet cut sharply on the jagged rocks and pieces of twigs, leaving drips of blood behind.

The animals above and below scurried away to shelter. Iracian quickened his pace until finally he came to a cliff covered with heather. There was a dark cave nearby and Iracian knew that the Pelican was in there.

"Hello, Pelican God," called Iracian.

"Come in, Iracian, I have been expecting you," said the Pelican God. "Let's see, you are here because your tribe is suffering of starvation, because the fish in the river have left you. Am I right?"

Iracian nodded his head.

"You have come here also to ask me for fish and ask me where the fish went off to."

"Yes," said Iracian quietly.

"Well, the fish went to a different lake. They wanted a tribe who only fished for what they needed. Your people seeemd to fish for more than you needed and filled yourselves so full of fish so often that the fish didn't want to fight for their life every single day." The Pelican's green eyes glared at Iracian while his long orange beak remained shut for some time.

Finally he nodded his big white feathery head and stood on his humanlike body flapping his wings. He walked around Iracian, he took each step with caution as if Iracian would try something.

"Okay, Iracian. I will make the fish go back only if you take what you need and go right now to apologize to the King Fish."

Once again Iracian started out on a long journey to the land of the fish.

When he got there he saw many fish swimming around the King Fish, who was sitting on a lily pad. Iracian went over to the fish.

"King Fish," he began, "I am sorry about the fish in our river. I'm Iracian, of the Shoshones. We are all starving because of the fish leaving us. Please bring them back, for we will only take what we need," he pleaded.

"Are you sure?" said the King Fish, "My young fish were very angry at your tribe."

"Yes, King Fish," said Iracian.

"Okay, I will let the fish back in."

That night Iracian returned home, with good news. The people were waiting patiently for Iracian to tell them.

That night the men went fishing for an hour, then returned home with a sack of fish. The tribe had a dance of thankfulness. They ate and rejoiced. But they only took what they needed.

UNDERSTANDING THE STORY

What preceded this final production? It all began with one reading group. They had finished a basal reader, and the teacher felt that they had been reading in a very mechanical fashion, without really thinking about the content of stories. Before starting the next basal, he decided to introduce legends and myths and encourage each group member to read independently. He was able to gather about sixty of the titles suggested in chapter seven, and the children began comparing the various legends.

During reading group time Mr. Booy taught story mapping, categorizing, and recognizing conflict and theme development, using the lesson suggestions in chapters two and three of this book. The children were most interested in comparing Native American tales with those from other cultures, and the study proceeded in that direction. The children never seemed to tire of mapping the stories.

During this time children wrote journal entries and made comparison charts and story maps to share with the group. Meanwhile, the rest of the class asked to be included, and the teacher began reading Native American legends and myths to the whole group. The artwork of the books was intriguing to the children and the class embarked on a study of Native American Art.

REINFORCING UNDERSTANDING

Earlier in the school year the class had studied trees. Now they became interested in trees as symbols and the Indian totems became very real to them. With the cooperation of the art teacher, the children planned to build their own totems. The class was divided into groups of three, and they began constructing their shapes from the scores of boxes the teacher collected from local merchants. Each one in the group of three picked one object to place on the pole, which they would later write about. Kathi picked the unicorn, Jill chose the salmon, and Katie chose the pelican.

Drawings of possible shapes and design were made on paper before the actual construction began. When the groups of three were satisfied with their plans, they began taping the boxes together, often reconstructing the boxes to fit their planned shapes. Much masking tape was used! Then the papier-mâché process began, a slow but inexpensive activity, with the use of brown paper toweling for the surface layer. The designs that the children had drawn on paper were now drawn with pencil on the totem, and painted with black paint. The final step was to add the color. The use of the textured paper toweling made it possible to leave some of the surface a barklike brown. The whole process took three months, with much of the work fitting into spare moments, recess, and lunch breaks.

WRITING WITH FOLK LITERATURE

Meanwhile, prewriting activities were leading up to the students writing their own legends to accompany the totems. The rereading of several short legends focused on types of characters, names of characters, common themes, and common conflicts. The picturesque and flowing language was noted. The day before the "serious writing" was going to begin, the groups spent an afternoon researching the Indian tribe or area that they had chosen to write about. This was to verify what they had learned from the legends

FIGURE 6.2. Each symbol on the totem was created and constructed by the children.

concerning the location, type of environment, habits, and animals of the region. Although this was not their favorite activity, the children recognized that the aura of a legend had to be established.

Now they were ready to plan their plot, conflict, theme, and characters to explain the object that they were designing on their totems. Story mapping served as an outline for their stories. They were very familiar with the process from mapping other authors' stories, and now used this skill to plan what they were going to write. The teacher stated that this was a very helpful step in the writing process. The map helped the writers maintain the flow of their stories, which took several sittings to complete.

Jill prepared the map shown in figure 6.3 before writing her story.

Children refined their stories by reading them to the other group members and receiving suggestions from them. The teacher edited, and met with each child for final revisions during independent work time.

Now came the most difficult part, in which the students would prepare their own stories for telling. Mr. Booy found that the step from writing to reading the stories was not too difficult, but telling the story in an animated, interesting manner was a big order for fifth and sixth graders. They proceeded to work through the following six steps:

1. The writer memorized his or her own story.
2. The writer read the story to a partner line by line and the partner recited the line with exaggerated expression.
3. The teacher modeled, telling a story using nonsense words, and asked the class to determine what the story was about by reading his gestures and voice intonations. Several children offered to tell their story using nonsense words and gestures, to practice animated telling.
4. Each group listened to other groups practice the story.
5. The groups told their stories to the class, and the class commented on clarity, pace, and use of gestures.
6. The groups told their stories and displayed their totem in another classroom. Only groups that passed the approval of the class could take their stories to another room.

All the groups eventually received approval from the class, and the whole school was enriched by the accomplishments of the fifth and sixth graders. Kevin, Nikki, and Scott brought their stories to the second grade. Each of them wrote about different tribes, rather than sharing stories about

FIGURE **6.3.** Jill's story map for her legend.

TITLE   "How the Salmon Came to the Willamette River"

SETTING   Where: A forest in Oregon
           When: 1800s
CHARACTERS   Who: Shoshone Indians
                      Nicka--the bear
                      Red One--the salmon
                      Naway--the Indian boy who lives
                              with the bear

PROBLEM: The Shoshone fish all the salmon out of the
Willamette River.   Naway, who has lived with the bear
since his parents died, tries to help.

RESOLUTION: Naway makes a clay fish and with Nicka's
special powers he makes it come alive and puts it into
the river where it produces 100 fish.   Naway makes the
people realize that if they ever destroy the fish
again the bear will kill them all.

ACTIONS: 1. The Shoshone fish all the fish out of the
               Willamette River.   The bear and boy see
               it.
            2. The boy makes a clay fish and the bear
               transforms it into a living fish.
            3. The bear puts it into the river where it
               turns into many fish.
            4. Naway preaches to the people never to
               fish all fish out of the river again or
               the Red One will never return.

---

one tribe. The teacher reported that Kevin was a fifth grader who that year advanced in learning more than any other child in the class. Here is his story:

THE MOON OWL

Long ago, in Cleveland, there was a forest. The name of the forest was called the Changwa forest because there was an Indian village in it with the Changwa Indians living there. The forest had many animals in it. Most of the animals were birds. It had loons, ducks, eagles, hawks. But one bird was quite different from all the others. This bird was the owl.

The reason the owl was so different from all the other birds was because he was always wondering about things. Each morning he would wake up wondering about something.

FIGURE 6.4
Kevin and Nicole set up their totem in grade two for a storytelling session.

One time he woke up wondering about something a little different than all the other things he worried about. He was wondering about the sky. He wondered why the sky was always brightly lit during the daytime but was dark and didn't have a light in it at night.

This puzzled all the other birds too. They decided that they should do something about it.

They all thought and thought about lighting the sky at night. Then they decided to have someone wash in the river of light. Then they could build a throne for that bird to sit on, high in the sky.

The birds though this was a wonderful idea, but who would do it? This, too, puzzled the birds until they agreed to let the owl who first got them into this do it.

So the owl flew high into the sky and then dove down all the way down to the bottom of the river of light. When he came back up, he was a new bird. The other birds decided to name him The Moon.

They tried out their moon that night. It worked! When the owl came back from his work, he slept all day.

That is still his schedule today. Working at night, lighting the sky, and sleeping during the day.

When asked for an evaluation of the experience, John Booy reported that he felt all the time devoted to this was worthwhile.

"No time was spent on pencil biting or staring into space," he reported. "By the time the legend writing began, the children had been saturated with Indian lore, and they didn't seem to tire of it."

He could see improvement in other writing the children were doing. They appeared to be more comfortable with writing assignments, and expressed themselves in writing more effectively than before the legend-writing experience. They continued to be avid readers, finding more folk literature, as well as books from other genres, in the library.

7
Recommended Books for Children

Children deserve high standards of artistry and authenticity in folk literature. All translators and retellers of folktales for juvenile audiences make adaptations from the original source. The adaptations fit into three categories: alteration of motif, alteration of mood, or literary simplification or elaboration. Each type of adaptation must be evaluated on the basis of how accurately the retelling reflects the oral storytelling tradition, how authentically the culture of the people is preserved, and how carefully the essence of the tale has been maintained.

ADAPTING FOLKTALES

Motifs are altered by softening the cruelty in the tale and by making happy or moralized endings. Characters are changed, with adults in the original tale sometimes depicted as children in the retelling, or the sex of the characters changed to include more women. Obscenities are removed, and motifs rearranged to improve the flow of the story.

Alterations of the mood of the story often take the form of softening the tale, or eliminating cultural and stylistic peculiarities. In the illustrations an artist may alter the mood either by design or out of ignorance of the culture depicted.

Literary simplification is accomplished by cutting back on description and using simplified vocabulary. Elaboration includes injecting dialogue or fleshing out a sparse story.

Some of these changes are necessary and helpful for making the tales readable by children. Other changes affect the validity of the story. The reader must decide if the version presented is indeed an authentic rendition of the oral, traditional tale.

CRITERIA FOR EVALUATING FOLKTALE VERSIONS

Margaret Read MacDonald in her doctoral dissertation presents the following questions that a reader can ask when evaluating the quality of literary versions of folktales for children:

1. Is information given regarding the tale's source, its teller, and its collection?
2. Is the version faithful to its source? How is it adapted?
3. Does it retain pacing, flow, linguistic playfulness, and imagery of the original?
4. Is the writing of exceptional quality?
5. Does it contain ethnic content such as images, songs, word play?
6. Are the format and illustrations artistic and appropriate?
7. Are illustrations historically and culturally accurate?
8. How does this version compare with other versions of the same tale?
9. What are the author's qualifications?
10. How do area specialists perceive this version?
11. What effect does this story have on the child? Does the story possess a depth of human feeling and the nature of joy to bring to the reader?

(1979, pp. 122, 123)

This chapter contains appraisals of 142 literary versions of folktales that meet MacDonald's guidelines for evaluation. Each book that tells one single tale is listed alphabetically by the name of the person who retold, translated, or adapted the story. The collections of folktales are listed by the editor or compiler of the volumes.

The appraisals include a brief summary of the theme or the plot of individual stories, or information about the content of stories in the collections. The country or origin of the tale is given. Suggestions are given for using the selection in the classroom, or a reference is made to an outstanding feature of the story. Generally, no recommendation is given as to the appropriate grade level for using the story because I believe that decision is a personal one to be made by the child, teacher, or librarian. The many dimensions of the folktale make the stories appropriate at a variety of age and grade levels.

FOLK LITERATURE APPRAISALS

An asterisk preceding an entry indicates that the book's illustrations are worthy of note. If no illustrator is given for an asterisked entry, the illustrations were done by the author.

*Aardema, Verna. (1981). *Bringing the rain to Kapiti Plain.* Illustrated by Beatriz Vidal. New York: Dial Press. [African]
This version of a tale from Kenya adds a cumulative refrain and the rhythm of "The House that Jack Built." The story structure supplies a framework for story writing. The repetition and picturesque language make this a favorite for reading aloud and chanting. The brilliant folk art illustrations set the mood for the inevitable rainstorm.

*Aardema, Verna. (1979). *The riddle of the drum, a tale from Tizapan, Mexico.* Illustrated by Tony Chen. New York: Four Winds Press. [Mexican]
Prince Tuzan meets swift runner Corrin Corran, archer Tirin Tiran, hearer Oyin Oyan, blower, Soplin Soplan, and eater Comin Comon. All help the prince to solve the riddle and perform other feats to win the princess. This hero tale of enchantment is a model of language patterning. Compare Prince Tuzan with the prince in *Firebird* (Russian) and with the warrior in *Legend of Scarface* (American Indian).

*Aardema, Verna. (1977). *Who's in rabbit's house?* Illustrated by Leo & Diane Dillon. New York: Dial Press. [African]
The Masai African tale, illustrated with actors wearing animal masks, is a good model for dramatization. The jackal, leopard, elephant, and rhinoceros offer unsuitable help for rabbit who tries to get the fearful creature out of his house. All are surprised at the identity of the occupant. Language patterns, use of repetition, and ideophones make this version appealing for oral reading and chanting.

*Aardema, Verna. (1975). *Why Mosquitoes buzz in people's ears.* Illustrated by Leo & Diane Dillon. New York: Dial Press. [African]
When King Lion calls a tribal council to see why Mother Owl doesn't wake the Sun, he finds a chain of blame sent from monkey (who killed baby owl) to crow to rabbit to python to iguana to mosquito. An agreement to punish mosquito satisfies Mother Owl, and the days follow their normal pattern once more. The pattern of language is noteworthy, and can be chanted by the audience when read aloud. The dramatic full-color illustrations won the Caldecott award.

Aesop. (1971). *Aesop's fables.* Translated by Gaynor Chapman. New York: Atheneum. [European]

A straightforward version of the fables, this is written in simple, modern English retaining the flavor of the literary. The collection includes sixteen of the more commonly known fables. Many have the moral stated, but in others it is strongly implied. This translation is a good model for extracting the theme from references within the story.

*Aesop. (1985). *Aesop's fables.* Selected and illustrated by Michael Hague. New York: Holt, Rinehart & Winston. [European]

Simple, lilting language characterizes this collection of thirteen tales. Each has the moral stated. To develop critical thinking, state the moral before reading the story, and ask the children to listen for the events that teach the lesson.

Aesop. (1966). *The fables of Aesop.* Retold by Joseph Jacobs and illustrated by David Levine. New York: Macmillan. [European]

This appealing collection of Aesop's fables is written simply enough for young readers to understand and with enough of the traditional language for them to appreciate. The preface by Joseph Jacobs and the afterword by Clifton Fadiman are worthwhile references for the teacher.

*Baker, Olaf. (1981). *Where the buffaloes begin.* Illustrated by Stephen Gammell. New York: Frederick Warne. [North American Indian]

Nawa, the wise Indian, was the voice that kept the legend alive. The beautiful language in this version of a Plains Indian tale captures the sights and sounds of the Prairie. The black-and-white sketches enhance the reader's impression of the revered animals and the vastness of the plains. Discuss the Indian regard for the buffalo.

Bang, Molly Garrett. (1976). *Wiley and the Hairy Man.* New York: Macmillan. [Regional United States]

If the Hairy Man can be fooled three times, he will never bother anyone again. Wiley and his mother work hard to find ways to outwit the Hairy Man. Wiley conquers his fear, confronts the Hairy Man, and proves that people can outwit evil through wisdom and caring for one another. The interesting, easy writing style makes this a favorite for independent reading.

*Baylor, Byrd. (1981). *A god on every mountain top.* Illustrated by Carol Brown. New York: Scribner's. [North American Indian]

Byrd Baylor presents a collection of myths and legends from various North American Indian tribes. The first two sections, "Beginnings" and "Changes," contain the myths. Legends comprise the remaining sections: "Power," "Magic," "Mystery and Dreams," "The Beings in the Mountains." Discuss tribal beliefs that the Indians pass on to their children and the importance of the environment to the Indians.

Baylor, Byrd. (1976). *And it is still that way.* New York: Scribner's. [North American Indian]

The introduction describes how the legends in the book were collected from Arizona Indian children at school. Baylor has written down the stories exactly as the Indian children remembered hearing them from their parents and grandparents. They are grouped into topics: Why animals are the way they are, Why our world is as it is, Great troubles and great heroes, People can turn into anything, Brother Coyote, Magic all around us. This collection provides a model for children recording family folklore.

*Belpré, Pura. (1972). *Dance of the animals.* Illustrated by Paul Galdone. New York: Frederick Warne. [Puerto Rican]
This is a single story from *The Tiger and the Rabbit.* The dog and the goat outwit the lion who invites them to a dance to eat them. Plays on words offer interesting examples for a language study. Lively illustrations help establish the personalities of the characters.

*Belpré, Pura. (1969). *Oté: A Puerto Rican Folktale.* Illustrated by Paul Galdone. New York: Pantheon. [Puerto Rican]
Oté's family is under the power of the near-sighted devil, but the tiniest one in the family saves them by remembering the words of the wise woman who weaves magic spells. Compare with *Duffy and the Devil.* Colorful drawings capture the humor of the story and the tropical setting.

Belpré, Pura. (1946). *The Tiger and the rabbit and other tales.* Illustrated by Kay Parker. Boston: Houghton Mifflin. [Central American]
Tales in this collection feature clever animals with human characteristics. Compare with stories in *The Knee-High Man* by Julius Lester. There are also wonder tales of people with traits such as greediness, stubbornness, and selfishness. Use to teach recognitition of theme.

*Belting, Natalie. (1965). *Calendar moon.* Illustrated by Bernarda Bryson. New York: Holt, Rinehart & Winston. [World]
A lunar calendar is based on sayings of various cultures concerning the passage of time. The poetic expressions originate from Canadian and North American Indians, and Asian, African, and Alaskan sources. The illustrations add delicate mood-setting for the poetry. A similar collection from Natalie Belting that has explanations of heavenly bodies as its theme is *The Stars Are Silver Reindeer.* (1966). Illustrated by Esta Nesbitt. New York: Holt, Rinehart & Winston.
Both books provide exquisite poetry models.

Belting, Natalie. (1965). *The earth is on a fish's back.* Illustrated by Esta Nesbitt. New York: Holt, Rinehart & Winston. [World]
Twenty-one myths and legends of "how things came to be" are collected here from various countries. Included are explanations of natural phenomena, such as "How men brought fire to earth" (Snake Indians, California) and "Why the sun is brighter than the moon" (Lilloit Indians of British Columbia), and basic skills, such as "How

spiders taught women to weave" (Chaco Indians of Argentina). The straightforward story lines, similar from country to country, offer a format for comparing these tales.

Belting, Natalie. (1961). *The long-tailed bear.* Illustrated by Louis F. Cary. New York: Bobbs-Merrill. [North American Indian]
These American Indian legends explain the origin of animal characteristics. The origin of each tale is credited to a particular Indian tribe. The stories are told briefly and simply, making them easy reading and good writing models. The predictable story pattern leads to a surprise ending.

*Belting, Natalie. (1974). *Whirlwind is a ghost dancing.* Illustrated by Leo & Diane Dillon. New York: Dutton. [North American Indian]
Indian motifs drawn with pastels and acrylics accentuate the imagery in the poems. Each poem is identified by tribal origin. The metaphors make word pictures of nature lore of the various tribes. Use to stimulate creative language usage.

*Bernstein, Margery, & Kobrin, Janet. (1976). *The first morning: An African myth.* Illustrated by Enid Warner Romanek. New York: Scribner's. [African]
A tale of the Sukuma people of East Africa begins with earth animals living in darkness. Lion has seen the light in the sky during a storm. Outwitting the Sky King, the Mouse, Fly, and Spider take the box of light back, and are surprised to find in it a rooster. Then the rooster "calls up the sun." The story illustrates the need to suspend judgment throughout the narrative, and to add one's own interpretation to the ending.

*Bernstein, Margery, & Kobrin, Janet. (1977). *The summer maker: An Ojibway Indian myth.* Illustrated by Anne Burgess. New York: Scribner's. [Canadian Indian]
Ojeeg the fisher and his animal friends go to the land above the mountain to find summer. A manitou tells them to crack open a hole in the sky and let the birds out. They succeed with difficulty and complications arise. Note the human characteristics of Ojeeg, the otter. Compare with *How Summer Came to Canada* by Willliam Toye.

*Bierhorst, John. (1978). *The girl who married a ghost and other tales from the North American Indian.* Photos by Edward S. Curtis. New York: Four Winds Press. [North American Indian]
An authentic collection of North American Indian tales is illustrated with beautifully reproduced photographs from writer-explorer Edward Curtis. Nine stories portray each major region inhabited by North American Indians. Types of stories include origin myth, wonder story, ghost story, and trickster animal tales. The photographs provide a link between the reality of the Indian's home and activities, and the mythical tales. Bierhorst captures Indian thought in his narrative, and his style challenges the sophisticated reader.

*Bierhorst, John. (1978). *The ring in the prairie.* Illustrated by Leo & Diane Dillon. New York: Dial Press. [North American Indian]
Originally set down by Henry Schoolcraft, this legend is in the poetic tradition of American Indian folklore. Hunter Waupee is intrigued by a strange circle in the prairie grass, and supernatural events begin. Legendary motifs include humans changing to animals, marriage of human with supernatural being, and use of charms. Poetic language and imagery are exemplary for language study.

*Bierhorst, John. (1984). *Spirit child.* Illustrated by Barbara Cooney. New York: Morrow. [Mexican]
Bierhorst translated an Aztec account of the birth of Christ. This version interweaves biblical stories, medieval legend, and traditional Aztec lore. The illustrations emulate Aztec art in a striking manner. Compare to the Bible story of the birth of Jesus.

*Brown, Marcia. (1972). *The bun.* New York: Harcourt Brace Jovanovich. [Russian]
This Russian nursery tale tells of baking a bun that comes alive and escapes to roll down the road, only to be eaten by a fox. See lesson plan comparing *The Bun, The Pancake,* and *The Gingerbread Boy* in chapter two of this book.

Brown, Marcia. (1961). *Once upon a mouse.* New York: Scribner's. [East Indian]
Marcia Brown tells this fable from ancient India using woodcuts and simple narrative. The old hermit reflects about big and little. When the mouse is changed to cat, dog, and then to tiger, he forgets his humble beginnings. The message can be understood at different levels of complexity depending on the developmental level of the reader. Can be used to demonstrate understanding of theme.

Bryan, Ashley. (1977). *The dancing granny.* New York: Atheneum. [West Indian]
Spider Ananse uses his clever trickery to get Granny Anika to dance away from her field so he can feed his family from her garden. Introduce this book to children who already know the African Anansi. This version is from the Antilles, and depicts the spider as a young man, whereas in African tales he is a spider man or an old man.

*Bryan, Ashley. (1971). *The ox of the wonderful horns and other African tales.* New York: Atheneum. [African]
Five stories: four trickster animal and one fairy tale. These stories are excellent short stories to use in teaching theme. The trickster animals are the frog, the hare, and the spider. All of these are admired by Africans for their cunning. Make charts to compare trickster traits.

*Carew, Jan. (1974). *The third gift.* Illustrated by Leo & Diane Dillon. Boston: Little, Brown. [African]
The Jubas are led by the prophet Amakosa to the foot of Nameless Mountain. Here

each new leader climbs the mountain to bring the clan a gift. The tribe receives work, beauty, and imagination from the consecutive leaders. In telling the story, Jan Carew demonstrates the gift of language with figurative expressions. The abundance of idioms and metaphor makes this a book to be read aloud with a discussion of the picturesque language.

Carey, Bonnie. (1973). *Baba Yaga's geese.* Illustrated by Guy Fleming. Bloomington: Indiana University Press. [Russian]
These Russian folktales are representative of the wide variety of Russian lore. Readers can evaluate the veracity of the stories by consulting the explanatory preface and the appendix, which cites sources. In many of the stories the theme is stated at the beginning, or at the end, and the reader can discover how the story unfolds the information needed to understand the theme.

Carpenter, Frances. (1949). *Tales of a Chinese grandmother.* Illustrated by Maithe Hasselriis. New York: Doubleday. [Chinese]
The grandmother of the Ling household is introduced in the first chapter. Each following chapter is a tale she tells her grandchildren. Conclusions concerning Chinese culture can be drawn from these stories. Offers a good model for collecting and recording folklore.

Carter, Dorothy. (1974). *Greedy Mariani.* Illustrated by Trina Hyman. New York: Atheneum. [West Indian]
In this collection the reader meets some of the same characters met in African cultures, with variations in actions and spelling (Annancy instead of Anansi) and episode, but similarities in personality. Personal characteristics of wisdom or stupidity, generosity or greediness, courage or cowardice win their just deserts in these tales from the Antilles.

Chase, Richard. (1948). *Grandfather tales.* Boston: Houghton Mifflin. [Regional American]
Tales commonly known through European collections appear here with the local color and dialect of the Appalachian settler. Compare the language and story line in these tales with other familiar versions. "The Old Sow and Three Shoats" is similar to "The Three Little Pigs," "Ashpet" resembles "Cinderella," and "Sody Sally-raytus" is like "Three Billy Goats Gruff."

Chase, Richard. (1950). *Jack and the three sillies.* Boston: Houghton Mifflin. [Regional American]
A regional United States tale of foolish Jack, whose swapping of his horse gets him a rock instead of the fifty dollars the horse is worth. His wife bets him that no man in the world is sillier. She does find three sillies, and in the process earns fifty dollars. Compare with Russian tales "The Falcon Under the Hat" and "Three Rolls and a Doughnut."

Chase, Richard. (1943). *The Jack tales.* Illustrated by Berkely Williams, Jr. Boston: Houghton Mifflin. [Regional United States]
These stories from Southern Appalachia with the style and humor of mountain folk are variants of English tales. Jack is a human hero who has fantastic adventures and always wins. Familiar themes include "Jack and the Bean Tree," and "Jack and the North West Wind." Draw conclusions about the character from the action of the story.

*Coalson, Glo. (1971). *Three stone woman.* New York: Atheneum. [Alaskan]
Read to the class to develop the use of setting and visual images for discovering un-stated premises in the story. An Eskimo tale of Ana, a starving widow who travels through the harsh Arctic cold to beg for food from her brother-in-law. Her sister-in-law removes the food given her and places three stones in her bag. Two super-natural strangers meet her and leave her a tiny sealskin bag which never empties of meat and blubber. A comparison of the literary version with the filmed version "Three Stone Blades" (Visual Americana, International Film Bureau) centers on visual impressions and the differences in story content.

*Coatsworth, Emerson, & Coatsworth, David. (1980). *The adventures of Nanabush: Ojibway Indian.* New York: Atheneum. [Canadian Indian]
These legends concern Nanabush, one of the most powerful manitous, or spirits, of the Ojibway world. He is both a provider and a trickster. Tales tell how and why things are as they are today as a result of either Nanabush's creativity or his trickery. Each tale is a model of the unique blending of the components of a legend, as handed down by the Canadian Indians. The preface gives interesting information about the collectors of the tales and the Indian illustrator.

Courlander, Harold. (1957). *The hat-shaking dance and other tales from the Gold Coast.* Illustrated by Enrico Arno. New York: Harcourt Brace Jovanovich. [African]
Twenty-one tales from Africa's Gold Coast include many tales about the Sky-God, Nyame. All the stories include Anansi. The first tale relates how all stories belong to Anansi and compares with *A Story, a Story* by Gail Haley. Many stories have counterparts in other cultures. For example, "Anansi Plays Dead" is similar to the "Tar Baby" story of Southern United States blacks. Notes beginning on page 103 in the book are helpful for understanding the Ashanti people.

Courlander, Harold. (1962). *The king's drum and other African stories.* Illustrated by Enrico Arno. New York: Harcourt Brace Jovanovich. [African]
These short, pointed tales have specific, usually stated, themes. Some, such as "The Search," end with a question that is impossible to answer, emphasizing the complexity of life. Other tales, such as "Past and Future" and "The Elephant Hunters," reveal conflicts settled through wisdom. African storytellers delight in tales of

human weakness ending with statements such as, "The great tree sees far but it falls loudly." Use to develop understanding and appreciation of metaphor.

Courlander, Harold. (1968). *Olode the hunter and other tales from Nigeria.* Illustrated by
    Enrico Arno. New York: Harcourt Brace Jovanovich. [African]
The subject of many tales is an animal trickster called Brother, who parallels Brother Terrapin in United States black folklore, and is a counterpart of the Ashanti Anansi. Three of the myths of the Ife tribe parallel Bible stories. An appendix provides explanations of the tales and gives comparisons with other cultures. The vocabulary of these tales is easy but the concepts are more complex than in the Ashanti tales or King's Drum stories.

Courlander, Harold. (1957). *Terrapin's pot of sense.* Illustrated by Elton Fax. New
    York: Holt, Rinehart & Winston. [Regional United States]
These rich Negro folktales collected from Alabama, New Jersey, and Michigan are written in Br'er Rabbit dialect. The themes of the various trickster tales can be recognized by juvenile readers through statements made by the storyteller or one of the main characters. Compare with Russian and African tales.

Courlander, Harold, & Hertzog, George. (1950). *The cow-tail switch and other West
    African stories.* Illustrated by MadyeLee Chastain. New York: Holt, Rinehart &
    Winston. [African]
Many of the African tales in this collection are remarkable for their play-on-words humor. Characters are given names that relate to the action of the story; one man is named Time, another called Nothing.

Courlander, Harold, & Leslau, Wolf. (1950). *The fire on the mountain and other Ethio-
    pian stories.* Illustrated by Robert Kane. New York: Holt, Rinehart &
    Winston. [African]
The wisdom and experience of the African man is related in these favorite tales of the Ethiopians. Most are told for the lessons in human behavior to be learned through the wisdom or foolishness, and pride or humility of the animals and men in the stories. The stories reflect the living conditions of the people and their race between floods and droughts. Reading these stories aloud can stimulate a thoughtful discussion.

*Crompton, Anne Eliot. (1975). *The winter wife: An Abenaki folktale.* Illustrated by
    Robert A. Parker. Boston: Little, Brown. [North American Indian]
The hunter is living alone, lonely and hungry. The events that lead him to take a winter wife and later a summer wife build up very predictably. The reader can make predictions but must wait for all the evidence before making judgments.

*Daniels, Guy. (1969). *The falcon under the hat: Russian merry tales and fairy tales.* Illus-
    trated by Feodor Rajankovsky. New York: Funk & Wagnalls. [Russian]
Explanation of the rich Russian oral tradition in the preface facilitates appreciation

of the tales. Daniels defines fairy tale as "a story involving faerie, or enchantment, serious in intent, which most often has a happy ending." The eleven stories are excellent examples of Russian lore. Many of the merry tales are based on the theme of the cleverness of peasants in tricking people in high places, such as "The Miser," "The Monastery of No Cares," and "Shemyaka the Judge." The harsh cruelty typical of some of the Russian fairy tales is evident in "The Magic Ring" and "The Snake."

*Daniels, Guy. (1970). *Foma the terrible.* Illustrated by Imero Gobbato. New York: Delacorte Press. [Russian]
Foma, a foolish Russian lad, killed twelve flies and left to prove his fame as a brave warrior. His adventures include conquering the Chinese army and marrying the Prussian princess. A good example of revealing a character through story action.

*d'Aulaire, Ingri, & d'Aulaire, Edgar. (1972). *D'Aulaire's trolls.* New York: Doubleday. [Norwegian]
Explanations of the trolls of Norway are given in expository style. Within the explanations are exemplary tales of a troll with twelve heads, a lumberjack troll and forest troll, and the boy who caught the eye shared by three trolls. The d'Aulaires's illustrations extend the text and set the mood for understanding these strange mountain folk.

*d'Aulaire, Ingri, & d'Aulaire, Edgar. (1969). *East of the sun and west of the moon.* New York: Viking Press. [Norwegian]
The magic of Norwegian forests, mountains, and valleys gives life to trolls, spirits, and beautiful princesses. In comparing these tales with fairy tales from China, Russia, or Africa, the distinctiveness of the setting stands out as does the universality of the motifs found in this beautiful collection.

*Demi. (1980). *Liang and the magic paintbrush.* New York: Holt, Rinehart & Winston. [Chinese]
A poor boy who longs to paint is given a magical paintbrush by a man who appears on a phoenix. Liang's gift brings joy to the common people, but devastation for the greedy emperor. The richly detailed watercolors offer a fine example of Chinese art.

*dePaola, Tomie. (1978). *The clown of God.* New York: Harcourt Brace Jovanovich. [Italian]
This Renaissance tale gives the modern reader a picture, both by word and illustration, of the society of old Italy. This version of the legend of the little juggler giving his talent to the Christ child is well suited for pantomime or creative dramatics.

*dePaola, Tomie. (1981). *Fin M'Coul: The giant of Knockmany Hill.* New York: Holiday House. [Irish]
This story takes an episode from the life of the popular Irish folklore giant. The il-

lustrations and rhythmical dialogue make this version an entertaining delight for children of all ages. *Fin M'Coul* is a good choice for creative dramatics or pantomime.

*dePaola, Tomie. (1980). *The Lady of Guadalupe, or Nuestra Señora de Guadalupe.* New York: Holiday House. [Mexican]
DePaola retells the legend of the appearance of the Lady to a poor farmer in Mexico in 1531. Since this edition is also printed in Spanish, the tale is a good choice for the bilingual classroom or in a unit about Mexico.

*dePaola, Tomie. (1975). *Strega Nona.* Englewood Cliffs, NJ: Prentice-Hall. [Italian]
Strega Nona and her magical pasta pot is a favorite folktale for young children. Big Anthony's dilemma can be depicted in dramatic play. With repeated readings, the children join in on the pasta pot rhymes. Tomie dePaola's illustrations resemble stage settings and provide ideas for making stage scenery.

*DeRoin, Nancy. (1975). *Jataka tales: Fables from the Buddha.* Illustrated by Ellen Lanyon. Boston: Houghton Mifflin. [East Indian]
These thirty fables were originally told by the Buddha five hundred years before Christ, according to legend. Similarities to Aesop's fables are apparent: animals speak and act, life situations require basic decisions, and the solutions are stated with morals. Differences appear in the underlying philosophy. The Jataka tales point to solutions to problems through recognizing the importance of the individual and the need to accept and understand the realities of life. Aesop's fables point to attempts to manipulate external forces and control or overcome enemies. Comparisons of the fables will enhance a study of theme with intermediate grade children.

*Dobbs, Rose. (1944). *No room: An old story retold.* Illustrated by Fritz Eichenberg. New York: David McKay. [Russian]
A Russian peasant is cured of his selfishness by following the advice of the Wise Man, ruler of the village. The repetition and suspense of the story will lead the reader to draw conclusions about the characters of the old man and the wise man as well as anticipate the sequence of episodes.

*Domanska, Janina. (1979). *King Krakus and the dragon.* New York: Morrow. [Polish]
A Polish legend tells how the town of Krakow was saved from the dragon through the ingenuity of a shoemaker's apprentice. The apprentice does not win the princess for his accomplishments, but rather becomes the court shoemaker. Questions will help direct a discussion: Did you predict a different ending? Why do you think the story ended this way? Striking illustrations include symbols on each page.

Durham, Mae. (1967). *Tit for tat and other Latvian folktales.* Illustrated by Harriet Pincus. New York: Harcourt Brace Jovanovich. [Southeastern European]

These Latvian stories can be identified by tale types that are found internationally. Many of the stories compare with the Russian *The Lazies*. Several devil stories can be compared with *Duffy and the Devil*, *Oté*, and "Shrewd Woman" from *Baba Yaga's Geese*.

Elliot, Geraldine. (1968). *The long grass whispers*. Illustrated by Sheila Hawkins. New York: Schocken. [African]
In the huts of the Ngoni people, grandmothers would tell about how animals live and talk in the long grass. "Her imagination has clothed them in her own speech" (p. vii). Word pictures drawn by Elliot in animal conversations and actions present a lively model for critical writing.

Finger, Charles. (1924). *Tales from silver lands*. Illustrated by Paul Honore. New York: Doubleday. [South American]
Finger relates the origin of many of the tales that he records. This is the most extensive collection of authentic South American tales available at present. "The Tale of the Gentle Folk" is a good one to read to the class as an example of how folktales were believed by the natives. One story that deals directly with the results of making judgments based on inadequate information is "The Tale That Cost a Dollar."

*Gackenbach, Dick. (1977). *The Leatherman*. New York: Seabury Press. [Regional United States]
The mood is set for this intriguing tale with an opening description of Ben's dream, in which a leather coat floats "like a ship from a fog," and Ben is "drowning in an ocean of molasses." Vivid word imagery characterizes this real life tale based on the travels of the eccentric Jules Bourelay, the Leatherman, who wandered the countryside of Connecticut in the mid 1880s. The line and wash drawings capture the feelings of the boy when he confronts the strange man.

Gag, Wanda. (1979). *The sorcerer's apprentice*. Illustrated by Margot Tomes. New York: Coward-McCann. [European]
The boy becomes an apprentice to the evil sorcerer under the pretense of being illiterate. In secret, he reads the sorcerer's book of spells and tricks. The good apprentice is able to win over the bad sorcerer, and prove that sorcery can be used for good as well as evil. The exemplary plot with an easily recognized theme, a quick introduction, suspense, logical development, and swift conclusion is a good model for writing.

*Galdone, Paul. (1975). *Billy goats gruff*. New York: Seabury Press. [Norwegian]
This version of the Billy goats gruff story pictures a very mean troll that alternately delights and frightens the young listener. Creative dramatic play, with the children providing their own words and actions, is an entertaining way to get preschoolers and kindergarteners responding to literature.

Galdone, Paul. (1975). *The gingerbread boy.* New York: Seabury Press. [United States]
Galdone retells the classic nursery tale in clear, easy to read, and literary style. The repetition of the gingerbread boy's chant, and the account of the many folk who run after him, make this a story that the beginning reader can soon read alone. The comical illustrations help tell the story and jog the reader's memory if a word or phrase is forgotten.

Galdone, Paul. (1968). *Henny-Penny.* New York: Seabury Press. [English]
Henny Penny is a cumulative animal tale. The repetition makes it a favorite with beginning readers. Other versions of this story are titled "Chicken Licken" or "Chicken Little." The plot and sequence of the story can be extended by having the young reader draw the animals, cut them out, and manipulate them in a retelling of the story.

Ginsburg, Mirra. (1973). *The lazies: Tales of the peoples of Russia.* New York: Macmillan. [Russian]
This collection of tales is based on the theme that indolence will bring no reward. The humorous tales include much folk wisdom and humor. By focusing on the variety of ways the theme is presented, the reader can be directed to an evaluation of plot structure.

Ginsburg, Mirra. (1973). *One trick too many.* Illustrated by Helen Siegl. New York: Dial Press. [Russian]
The trickster animal of Russia is the fox, and his tales are beautifully told by Mirra Ginsburg as collected and translated from her own childhood in Russia. At times the fox knows when to stop his tricks, but at other times his cleverness gets him into trouble. This collection contains stories that fit each of the subgroups of animal tales. The woodcuts, printed in yellow, red, and black, and framed with symbolic animal and plant forms, depict scenes from the tales.

Ginsburg, Mirra. (1974). *The proud maiden, Tungak, and the sun.* Illustrated by Igor Galanin. New York: Macmillan. [Russian Eskimo]
The legend tells how the moon came to live in the sky and why the long Arctic night gives way to a long Arctic day. A hunter's proud daughter escapes the evil spirit of the tundra and marries the sun. The blending of natural and supernatural beings and the logical but fantastic explanation of natural phenomena make this story a good example of the legend category of folk literature.

Ginsburg, Mirra. (1975). *Three rolls and one doughnut.* Illustrated by Anita Lobel. New York: Dial Press. [Russian]
The varied characters and the way their problems are amusingly resolved in the legends, fables, and riddles of this collection depict Russian people as part of the universal heritage of folk culture and as persons with humor and wisdom. These

stories were collected and translated from Mirra Ginsburg's childhood in Russia. Her concise direct style provides easy reading.

*Goble, Paul. (1984). *Buffalo Woman*. New York: Macmillan. [North American Indian]

The buffalo was a source of life for the Plains Indians. This tale varied from tribe to tribe, but always was used to teach that the buffalo and the people were related. The intent was to strengthen the bond with the herds and to encourage the buffalo to give of himself for the people. Goble's highly stylized drawings portray the power and force of the buffalo, and picture the close bond between buffalo and Indian. Discussion of this book with intermediate grade children can help develop an understanding of Indian culture.

*Goble, Paul. (1983). *Star Boy*. Scarsdale, NY: Bradbury Press. [North American Indian]

Goble's exquisite, brilliant drawings combine with clear, literary language to make this version of "Star Boy" ("Scarface") a fascinating story of the Sky World. Within the story, which is worthy of enjoying on its own merit, one also learns why the Blackfeet dance the Sun Dance, a ceremonial thanksgiving to their Creator. Legendary information about the Evening and Morning Star is given. *Star Boy* provides background information that enhances the reading of San Souci's *The legend of Scarface*.

*Grimm, Jacob & Wilhelm. (1981). *Cinderella*. Illustrated by Nonny Hogrogian. New York: Greenwillow. [German]

This version of Cinderella uses a hazel tree, planted by Cinderella, and a white dove as tools of enchantment rather than a fairy godmother and a pumpkin. Lovely, powerful artwork enhances the tale. Compare with other European versions as well as the Chinese and Vietnamese stories. See Perrault, Louie, and Vuong entries in this chapter.

*Grimm, Jacob & Wilhelm. (1980). *The fisherman and his wife*. Translated by Randall Jarrell and illustrated by Margot Zemach. New York: Farrar, Straus & Giroux. [German]

Picturesque language and an abundance of conversation characterize this charming version of a familiar folktale. The greedy woman and the simple fisherman are pictured in their changing environment with both humor and imagination. This is a good story for children to illustrate from their own visual images before Zemach's drawings are shared. The vivid description of the sea is worthy of note.

*Grimm, Jacob & Wilhelm. (1974). *Snow White*. Translated by Paul Heins and illustrated by Trina Hyman. Boston: Little, Brown. [German]

For the child who has heard only the Walt Disney version of Snow White, this story will be a surprise. The oral tradition of the story and the translation based on the early written version should be explained to the listener or child reader. The reader should be at least eight years or older if he or she is to understand the fantasy of this story. The illustrations portray a dark and foreboding German forest, realistically interpreting the setting of the tale.

*Grimm, Jacob & Wilhelm. (1972). *Snow White and the seven dwarfs.* Translated by Randall Jarrell and illustrated by Nancy Burkert. New York: Farrar, Straus & Giroux. [German]

The text, as translated by Randall Jarrell, is similar to the translation by Paul Heins. The main difference is in the illustration. Nancy Burkert's forest and dwarfs are less foreboding than those of Trina Hyman. The kingdom appears as a magical, mythical world. A comparison of and open discussion about the feelings that different illustrations evoke assist the readers in evaluating the stories.

*Hague, Kathleen, & Hague, Michael. (1980). *East of the sun and west of the moon.* Illustrated by Michael Hague. New York: Harcourt Brace Jovanovich. [Norwegian]

This complex story was a favorite of the girls in a sixth grade class. It includes many characteristics of a classical fairy tale: a broken promise, supernatural feats, a quest. All this is accomplished by a girl who wins the prince rather than a boy who wins the princess. Mystical illustrations extend the story. Compare with d'Aulaire's version.

Haley, Gail. (1970). *A story, a story.* New York: Atheneum. [African]
Anansi wants the Sky-God's stories and succeeds in accomplishing the three feats required to win the treasure. This version can be read by a child with limited ability because of the predictable style and repetition.

Harris, Christie. (1977). *Mouse woman and the mischief makers.* Illustrated by Douglas Tait. New York: Atheneum. [Canadian Indian]
As a supernatural being called Narnauk, Mouse Woman guarded the seas and wilderness of Canada's northwest coast. Anyone disturbing the order of this part of the world was a mischief maker, and Mouse Woman would deal with him! Most of the tales are concerned with humans desiring what they should not have and misusing natural resources. The stories end with some variant of "no good ever comes of upsetting the proper order of the world." Provides a good introduction to a study of ecology.

Harris, Christie. (1976). *Mouse woman and the vanished princess.* Illustrated by Douglas Tait. New York: Atheneum. [North American Indian]
The library card summary labels these stories legends. However, the reader will find many characteristics of fairy tales in the adventures of the Indian princesses who are carried away by supernatural forces and rescued through great adventures, each one assisted by Mouse Woman.

Harris, Christie. (1973). *Once more upon a totem.* Illustrated by Douglas Tait. New York: Atheneum. [North American Indian]

The art form of the symbolic totem comes alive in the expressive imagery of Harris in three celebrated stories from the potlatch feasts. The use of figurative language captures the mystery of nature that permeates the Indian beliefs. A discussion of "the people who owned the stories" is a fitting culmination to the study of folk literature.

Harris, Christie. (1963). *Once upon a totem.* Illustrated by John Frazer Mills. New
　　　York: Atheneum. [North American Indian]
A totem pole was usually raised to honor a particular chief, living or dead. The story behind each crest tells how one of the symbols came to be the emblem of a mythical ancestor. "The One Horned Mountain Goat" is the same story told by Toye in "Mountain Goats of Temlaham." Compare the storytellers' use of language.

Harris, Joel Chandler. (1955). *The complete tales of Uncle Remus.* Compiled by Richard
　　　Chase and illustrated by Arthur Frost. Boston: Houghton Mifflin. [Regional
　　　United States]
The stories of Br'er Rabbit as told by Joel Harris is written in dialect that needs much practice before it can be read to a group. The dialogue and unusual expressions make a fascinating word study of an individual project.

Hill, Kay. (1965). *Badger, the mischief maker.* Illustrated by John Hanberger. New
　　　York: Dodd, Mead. [North American Indian]
Glooscap watches over Badger's mischief making, knowing that Badger has a lot to learn. He finally does learn that to "be good from choice is the only safe way for then the joy is in the act itself and neither man nor god can withhold it" (p. 42). Badger learns this lesson the hard way, but he doesn't lose his spirit. Compare with Coyote, Rabbit, or Anansi, tricksters from other countries.

*Hodges, Margaret. (1972). *The fire bringer.* Illustrated by Peter Parnall. Boston: Lit-
　　　tle, Brown. [North American Indian]
The Paiute Indians tell how Boy was told by Coyote that with the help of one hundred swift runners they could get fire to keep people warm and help them cook their food. The runners form a relay to pass the fire from Burning Mountain to their caves. The Indians' questions concerning fire demonstrate the need to suspend judgment. The reader learns how difficult it is to understand an idea without background experience.

*Hodges, Margaret. (1984). *Saint George and the dragon.* Illustrated by Trina Schart
　　　Hyman. Boston: Little, Brown. [England]
Caldecott Medal–winning illustrations present a stunning picture of the English medieval countryside. Hodges retells a segment of a legend immortalized in Spenser's *The Faerie Queene.* George slays the dreadful dragon and brings peace to the land. This is an excellent choice for puppetry, drama, or reader's theater.

*Hoge, Dorothy. (1966). *The black heart of Indri.* Illustrated by Janina Domanska.
　　　New York: Scribner's. [Chinese]

Indri, the son of a water sprite and the prince of the toads, is the keeper of the water of life. Indri is unhappy because he is ugly and has a black heart. The water sprite tells him that he only thinks his heart is black: "If you will live for nine days in the presence of virtue, your ugliness will vanish." This becomes the task of the story. As the readers follow Indri's adventures, they can determine what will lead to the end of his predicament. Compare to frog prince and princess stories of Germany (Grimm) and of Russia (Whitney's *In a Certain Kingdom*).

*Hogrogian, Nonny. (1971). *One fine day.* New York: Macmillan. [Armenian]
This is a cumulative nursery tale in which the fox makes a number of bargains before getting his tail back from the old woman. Young children can chant the refrain, draw pictures in sequence, or improvise a presentation of this story.

Houston, James. (1972). *Songs of dream people.* New York: Atheneum. [Alaskan]
The vitality and force of the language of these Indian and Eskimo songs come from their origin as survival cries and work chants. The songs possess "an endless search for the magic of life." Should be read to the children with a musical accompaniment.

Houston, James. (1965). *Tikta'liktak: An Eskimo legend.* New York: Harcourt Brace
    Jovanovich. [Alaskan Eskimo]
This legend is a survival tale of a young hunter who is carried to sea on an ice floe. The mood is set in the first few pages with a description of Tikta'liktak's life and environment. Through skillful and powerful use of language, the author builds suspense as Tikta'liktak reaches such a state of hunger that he builds himself a coffin out of rocks and lies down to die. But Tikta'liktak receives new determination and inspiration, and fights his way back to his family. The story is developed through description and narrative, with no dialogue, and will be appreciated by an advanced reader.

Houston, James. (1967). *The white archer: An Eskimo legend.* New York: Harcourt
    Brace Jovanovich. [Alaskan Eskimo]
An exciting, dramatically written adventure story tells of Kungo, the twelve-year-old Eskimo, who seeks revenge for the death of his parents and capture of his sister by Indians in Alaska. Kungo's determination to be a great archer leads him to Ittok, who lives on a distant island. Kungo learns much from the wisdom and kindness of Ittok and his wife. The beautiful imagery and language make this book a literary experience as well as a satisfying adventure. This is recommended for an individual-directed reading-thinking activity for an advanced reader who would evaluate Kungo's experience and recognize his growth through his adventures and relationship with virtuous people.

*Hou-tien, Chieng. (1980). *Six Chinese brothers: An ancient tale.* New York: Holt,
    Rinehart & Winston. [Chinese]

The strength of the Chinese family is portrayed by six sons, each using their supernatural physical power to save first their father's life, and then their brothers' lives. They win the favor of the king. In contrast to the ethnically demeaning version by Clair Bishop, illustrated by Kurt Wiese, this version, with delicate scissors-cut illustrations by Chinese artists is an uplifting image of the Chinese.

Jagendorf, Moritz. (1968). *Ghostly folktales.* Illustrated by Oscar Liebman. Morristown, NJ: Silver Burdett. [World]
Ghost stories from many places in the world make intriguing reading for Halloween. The ghostly tales were popular, with "The Tale of the Hairy Toe" and "The Coffinmaker's Ghost Party" favorites of many sixth graders. Students in a sixth grade class made posters with the message of their favorite scary story for Halloween.

Johnson, Edna; Sickels, Evelyn; Sayers, Frances; & Horovitz, Carolyn. (1977). *Anthology of children's literature* (5th ed., part 3, pp. 259–725). Boston: Houghton Mifflin. [World]
A section on oral tradition in this anthology includes a wide selection of fables, animal tales, fairy tales, myths, legends, and epics collected from authentic translations dated in the 1800s and early 1900s. The Norwegian version of *The Pancake* used in the lesson in chapter three is included in this collection.

Jones, Hettie. (1974). *Coyote tales.* Illustrated by Louis Mafsie. New York: Holt, Rinehart & Winston. [North American Indian]
Four stories have been selected by the author to show the different aspects of Coyote's character. The reader can draw conclusions about how Coyote is revealed in each story: as a hero, as a trickster, with supernatural power, or making humanlike mistakes.

*Jones, Hettie. (1972). *Longhouse winter.* Illustrated by Nicholas Gaetano. New York: Holt, Rinehart & Winston. [North American Indian]
These tales should be told only in the winter, following the tradition of the Iroquois Indians. The book contains four stories with themes relating to the Indians' bond with their environment. Highly stylized geometric watercolors create the mood for the setting in these stories.

*Jones, Hettie. (1971). *The trees stand shining.* Illustrated by Robert Parker. New York: Dial Press. [North American Indian]
Songs of the American Indians that reveal their feelings about the world and their lives are translated from the various Indian languages by Hettie Jones. Direct poetic statements and impressionistic drawings combine to give the reader an understanding of the American Indian.

*Kirkup, James. (1973). *The magic drum.* Illustrated by Vo Dinh. New York: Knopf. [Chinese]

Tenko, "drum from heaven," is the god-given son of an aging peasant couple, Ohaku and Olo. They recognize the mysterious nature of this gift, and try to keep drums away from Tenko, fearing that the promise of the drum that announced his coming will also take him away. Their fears are realized. The story, based on a drama of the ancient tale performed in Japan, is delicately and simply told. Both the art and the drama style stimulate creative response.

*La Fontaine, Jean de. (1954). *The fables of La Fontaine.* Collected and adapted by
     Marianne Moore. New York: Viking Press. [European]
La Fontaine's fables are based on Aesop's collection. The delicate illustrations add to their appeal and interpretation. The use of dialogue makes these versions appealing to the reader and appropriate for dramatizing.

Leach, Maria. (1974). *Whistle in the graveyard: Folktales to chill your bones.* Illustrated by
     Kenn Rinciari. New York: Macmillan. [World]
From all over the world traditional tales about ghosts are collected here and classified by types of ghosts. Introduction gives background; notes and bibliography give sources and motifs. The very short stories capture the interest of the reluctant reader.

*Le Gallienne, Eva. (1982). *Legend of the Milky Way.* New York: Holt, Rinehart &
     Winston. [Chinese]
The first written version of this tale appeared in the *Book of Odes,* collected by Confucius in the fifth century B.C. The Queen Mother of the heavens separates the heavenly weaver princess from her earth husband, the flute player, by making them into stars. On the seventh day of the seventh month of the Chinese year, the princess, now the star Vega, goes across the silver river to visit her husband, Altair. A map of the constellations at the back of the book can stimulate the reader to learn more about stories behind the stars. MacDonald's *The Storyteller's Source Book* lists other folktales that explain astronomy.

Lester, Julius. (1972). *The knee-high man and other tales.* Illustrated by Ralph Pinto.
     New York: Dial Press. [Regional United States]
Six animal stories from American slave lore include trickster tales of Mr. Rabbit and Mr. Bear, familiar characters in black folktales, and the pourquoi tale "Why Waves Have Whitecaps." A good collection to read aloud for demonstrating the distinctiveness of animal tales, and distinguishing between the trickster tale, the pourquoi tale, and the fable.

*Lin, Adet. (1961). *The Milky Way and other Chinese folktales.* Illustrated by Enrico
     Arno. New York: Harcourt Brace Jovanovich. [Chinese]
The universal themes in these tales are developed with unique treatment of supernatural events. Many of the stories deal with humans marrying spirits of sky or water, such as the "Milky Way" and the "Boy Who Played the Flute." These stories can be compared with Indian tales collected by Natalie Belting in *the Long-tailed Bear*

or by the Raskins in *Indian Tales.* The tales of foolishness can be compared with Russian or United States stories.

*Louie, Ai-Ling. (1982). *Yeh Shen.* Illustrated by Ed Young. New York: Philomel. [Chinese]
This version of Cinderella is translated as it appeared in the *Miscellaneous record of Yu Yang,* a book which dates from the T'ang dynasty (A.D. 618–907). The oldest European version of Cinderella was an Italian tale, published in 1634. Young's lovely artwork repeats the fish motif on nearly every page, providing picturesque foreshadowing of the plot. A comparison of the Chinese and European Cinderellas will show marked similarities and differences in the two versions.

*McDermott, Beverly Brodsky. (1976). *The golem: A Jewish legend.* Philadelphia: Lippincott. [European]
Brilliant gouache, watercolor, dye, and ink drawings enhance this fine version of the legend recalled from the Jewish ghetto of Prague, Czechoslovakia. Recommended for critical discussion with older children (9–12). The quotation that prefaces the book can direct the attention of the listeners and stimulate a discussion of beliefs. This legend presents the idea that man cannot be like God. Whatever man creates can never match God's creation.

*McDermott, Gerald. (1977). *Anansi the spider.* New York: Holt, Rinehart & Winston. [African]
This story is typical of the multidimensional African folktales that reveal universal beliefs and parallel tales from other countries. Anansi goes on a long journey and is saved from disaster by his sons, each of whom uses his special ability as suggested by his name: See Trouble, Road Builder, River Drinker, Game Skinner, Stone Thrower, and Cushion. Compare with *Riddle of the Drum* by Verna Aardema and *Six Chinese Brothers* by Chieng Hou-tien.

*McDermott, Gerald. (1974). *Arrow to the sun.* New York: Viking Press. [North American Indian]
This Pueblo Indian myth is analogous to the Bible story of Christ's birth. Mocked by others because he doesn't know his father, Boy sets out on a search that leads to the Sun Lord. He passes through four chambers of ceremony to prove his birthright. Colorful, symbolic graphic designs are intriguing to intermediate grade children.

*McDermott, Gerald. (1984). *Daughters of the earth.* New York: Delacorte Press. [Roman]
This myth, which explains the origin of the seasons, is based on Ovid's *Metamorphoses.* Ceres is the Roman goddess of vegetation. Her beloved daughter, Proserpina, is kidnapped by Pluto, and taken to the underworld. In her absence, Ceres withdraws to a cave, and the world becomes barren. Jupiter orders Pluto to release Proserpina, but since she has eaten three seeds of a pomegranate, she has to return to the underworld for three months of the year. The book features vivid, emotionally

strong artwork and dramatic language. Compare with the Indian myth in the version by William Toye, *How Summer Came to Canada*. Use for art and language appreciation.

*McDermott, Gerald. (1975). *The stonecutter*. New York: Viking Press. [Japanese]
Tasaku becomes discontented as a lowly stonecutter, and the spirit of the mountain grants his wish to become a prince. As further discontent leads to further wishes, Tasaku comes to understand too late, the value of his position as stonecutter. McDermott made a film of this legend before writing the book (Weston Woods Studios). A comparison of the film and the book can lead to a discussion by intermediate grade children about what each medium contributes to the emotional impact of the message, and to an understanding of the theme.

*McDermott, Gerald. (1980). *Sunflight*. New York: Four Winds Press. [Greek]
McDermott provides an authentic, though abbreviated, interpretation of the myth of Daedalus and Icarus. Daedalus, the master craftsman, engineers the escape of himself and his son from the wicked king, Minos. However, the escape ends in tragedy because Icarus does not obey his father. Some basal readers contain abridged versions of this legend. Read McDermott's version for a comparison. The colorful symbolic illustrations help to interpret the mood of the story and add dignity to the narration.

*McGovern, Ann. (1969). *Hee haw*. Illustrated by Eric Von Schmidt. Boston: Houghton Mifflin. [Southern European]
In this version of Aesop's fable the donkey runs to freedom braying, "Hee-haw." The illustrations add both humor and a sense of the setting for a story of long ago. The repetitive language provides language encounters for young children. The theme is obvious, though unstated.

Maher, Ramona. (1969). *The blind boy and the loon and other Eskimo myths*. New York: John Day. [Alaskan Eskimo]
Survival in the harshness of the Eskimo world is the dominant theme of many of the animal tales and fairy tales in this collection. Specific aspects of survival themes are developed, such as the search for food ("How Thunder and Lightning Came to Be," "The Blind Boy and the Loon"), fighting for existence ("The Man Who Killed the Sea Monster," "The Hardhearted Rich Man"), and the breaking of taboos ("Moon Husband," and "Man Who Married a Snow Goose").

*Melzcak, Ronald. (1967). *The day Tuk became a hunter and other Eskimo stories*. Illustrated by Carol Jones. New York: Dodd, Mead. [Alaskan Eskimo]
These short exciting Eskimo tales contain characteristics of legend common to all cultures. They are distinctively Eskimo and provide a picture of life and beliefs of the Arctic.

*Melzcak, Ronald. (1970). *Raven, creator of the world.* Illustrated by Laszlo Gal. Boston: Little, Brown. [Alaskan Eskimo]
Eskimo explanations of the origins of the world, animals, and people take form in Raven stories told with simplicity and an understanding of Eskimo beliefs. These stories can be compared with Bible stories, North American Indian, and African myths. Imaginative two-color drawings help interpret the settings of the stories.

*Mikolaycak, Charles. (1984). *Babushka: An old Russian folktale.* New York: Holiday House. [Russian]
This traditional legend tells the story of an old lady who declines an invitation to meet the Christ Child. She spends the rest of her life searching for him and leaving gifts for children all over the world. The brilliantly painted illustrations show the changing seasons, the passing of years, and different countries that she visits. The artwork offers a striking example of how pictures enrich and enlarge a story.

*Mosel, Arlene. (1968). *Tikki tikki tembo.* Illustrated by Blair Lent. New York: Holt, Rinehart & Winston. [Chinese]
The Chinese have given all their children short names ever since the near tragedy of this "first and honored" son Tikki tikki tembo-no sa rembo-chari bari ruchi-pip peri pembo. Finely drawn illustrations add humor to this excellent version of a favorite legend. Elements of this story fit well into the definition of legend.

*Ness, Evaline. (1969). *Long, Broad and Quick-Eye.* New York: Scribner's. [Southeastern Europe]
The prince sets off to rescue a beautiful girl who is under the power of a wizard in an iron castle. On the way he meets Long, who will stretch to the sky; Broad, who can make himself wide; and Quick-Eye, who must bandage his eyes because they are so piercing that they destroy whatever he gazes upon. With their help, the prince accomplishes the three necessary tasks to free the princess. Compare with Russian *The Fool of the World* by Arthur Ransome, and Mexican *Riddle of the Drum* by Verna Aardema.

Newell, Edythe W. (1970). *The rescue of the sun, and other tales from far north.* Illustrated by Frank Altschuler. Chicago: Albert Whitman. [Alaskan Eskimo]
The first five stories give information about the children of the Far North and how they lived long ago. The stories that follow give evidence that cold and darkness are important factors in Eskimo explanations and adventures. An excellent reference for confirming hypotheses about why Eskimo tales deal with survival.

*Otsuka, Yuzo. (1981). *Suho and the white horse.* Illustrated by Suekichi Akaba. New York: Viking Press. [Chinese-Mongolian]
This legend is retold with beautiful literary language that captures the feelings of the boy and his love for the beautiful horse. After grieving, Suho conquers his sorrow, and makes a new kind of musical instrument from the bones of the horse, as he was

commanded in a dream. The mood-setting watercolor illustrations help the reader picture the wide expanse of the desolate Mongolian countryside. The reading of this legend could be accompanied by music simulating the sound of the Mongolian horsehead fiddle.

*Perrault, Charles. (1976). *Cinderella, or The little glass slipper.* Illustrated by Erol Le-
    Cain. Harmondsworth, Eng.: Puffin. [French]
This French version of Cinderella has stylistic, ethereal illustrations. It includes a fairy godmother as the source of enchantment, with the transformed pumpkin and mice for the coach and horses. The discerning reader will enjoy a comparison of both illustrations and text with versions from other countries. See *Cinderella* by Hogrogian and *Yeh Chen* by Ai-Ling Louie. Over three hundred versions of "Cin-derella" have been recorded. (See also Charles Perrault. (1985) *Cinderella.* Retold by Amy Ehrlich and illustrated by Susan Jeffers. New York: Dial Press)

*Ransome, Arthur. (1968). *The fool of the world and the flying ship.* Illustrated by Uri
    Shuleviz. New York: Farrar, Straus & Giroux. [Russian]
Fool is kind to an old man. The old man changes his poor food into a feast, and gives Fool instructions for finding a supernatural flying machine. Fool follows his advice to the letter, and flies over the countryside, picking up people he meets. Each of his passengers possesses special gifts that help the Fool perform feats necessary to win the Czar's daughter. God loves simple folk, and turns things to their advantage in the end.

*Raskin, Joseph, & Raskin, Edith. (1969). *Indian tales.* Illustrations by Helen Siegl.
    New York: Random House. [North American Indian]
Some of the same legends told in *The Long-tailed Bear* by Natalie Belting appear in this collection in a more detailed narrative. Many of the stories are developed through interwoven episodes that lead to a pointed conclusion. For example, "Why Animals Do Not Talk," presents the point of view of each animal in relation to man, and finally the Great Spirit intervenes to settle their arguments. The reader must suspend judgment until near the end of the story when all pieces fit together. The woodcuts, printed in green, black, and white, are of more subtle design that those in *One Trick Too Many* by Mirra Ginsburg.

Robinson, Gail, & Hill, David. (1976). *Coyote the trickster.* Illustrated by Graham
    McCollum. New York: Crane, Russak. [Canadian Indian]
The trickster character in Indian legend is an animal-god whose powers often help save man and other animals. On the other hand, being a complex character, the trickster can cause problems. The discerning reader of these well told legends can decide how the storyteller leads him to understand the trickster. The logical unfold-ing of the plot makes the story believable.

*San Souci, Robert. (1978). *The legend of Scarface.* Illustrated by Dan San Souci. New
    York: Doubleday. [North American Indian]

Scarface is ridiculed by his peers for his appearance and his poverty. He undertakes an adventurous trip to the sun and is successful because of his kindness to all whom he encounters. Read to the class as an example of how a legend unfolds. This story leads the reader to draw conclusions through a predictable plot. *Star Boy*, retold by Paul Goble, provides background for this episode.

Scheer, George F. (1968). *Cherokee animal tales.* Illustrated by Robert Frankenberg. New York: Holiday House. [North American Indian]
This outstanding collection of animal tales can be read by the less able reader in intermediate grades. The interesting, brief stories give clear explanations of natural phenomena. The reader can discover traits of the Cherokee Indian.

Silverman, Maida. (1984). *Anna and the seven swans.* Illustrated by David Small. New York: Morrow. [Russian]
This story appeals to young children, and is a less scary introduciton to Baba Yaga than other tales cited in this chapter. The lively illustrations help verify the magic in the tale. Anna is able to save her brother because Baba Yaga is helpless in the presence of love and caring.

*Singer, Isaac Bashevis. (1967). *Mazel and Shlimazel, or The milk of the lioness.* Illustrated by Margot Zemach. New York: Farrar, Straus & Giroux. [Russian]
A Russian folktale concerned with the war between good and evil. Mazel would bring happiness to the poorest of the village for one year, then Shlimazel would try to undo what Mazel had done in one second. The story is characterized by superb use of language and an intriguing weaving of the plot. The plot structure will help the reader make judgments about the good and evil forces in the story.

Singer, Isaac Bashevis. (1968). *When Shlemiel went to Warsaw and other stories.* New York: Dell. [Russian]
"Shrewd Todie and Lyser the Miser," "The Elders of Chelm and Genendel's Key," and "When Shlemiel Went to Warsaw" are stories in this collection that deal with amiable fools who convince the town wise men that their actions are logical. In addition to enjoying the stories for their humor and the Russian regard for the foolish man, Singer's use of figurative language and imagery offers language experience.

*Sleator, William. (1970). *The angry moon.* Illustrated by Blair Lent. Boston: Little, Brown. [Alaskan Indian]
Man and friendly supernatural forces can overcome the strong, angry forces. Lapowinsa laughs at the moon and the moon takes her up to his home. Lupan, through his ingenuity and courage, gets to the sky and meets a friendly grandmother. She gives him four magic gifts that he uses to stop the angry moon. Note how the illustrations help develop the theme.

*Small, Ernest. (1966). *Baba Yaga.* Illustrated by Blair Lent. Boston: Houghton Mifflin. [Russian]

The character of Baba Yaga is developed through stories about Marusia, who is captured by Baba Yaga, and stories about a hedgehog who is really a boy who has been enchanted by the black sunflower that Baba Yaga is seeking. Baba Yaga is portrayed as a horrible but basically harmless witch who is easily influenced but hard to escape from completely. This caricature of Baba Yaga should be compared with other authors' renditions for evaluation of character development.

Stoutenberg, Adrien. (1968). *American tall tale animals.* Illustrated by Glen Rounds. New York: Viking Press. [Regional United States]
The names of the "Strange animals lolloping around in the early days of our country" arouse the curiosity of the reader of these fantastic stories collected from throughout the United States. The colloquialisms of the various regions and the picturesque language can be appreciated by the discerning reader.

Sturton, Hugh. (1966). *Zomo the rabbit.* Illustrated by Peter Warner. New York: Atheneum. [African]
Hausa people of Africa tell stories of Zomo the Rabbit, the trickster who always wins even when he loses. Notes by the publisher explain the changes made in translation from the early sources. Children recording family tales can refer to this explanation for editing ideas.

Tolstoy, Alexei. (1968). *The great big enormous turnip.* Illustrated by Helen Oxenbury. London: William Heinemann. [Russian]
This simple cumulative tale tells of the need for teamwork. Everyone from grandpa to the mouse is needed to pull up the turnip. The message and the story patterns make this book an excellent choice for dramatic play, chanting, and sequence pictures.

*Towle, Faith. (1975). *The magic cooking pot.* Boston: Houghton Mifflin. [East Indian]
This version of a favorite Indian folktale is illustrated with batik. The illustrations are made with the traditional Indian colors yellow, orange, red, maroon, and black. The story is about a poor religious man who is given two magic cooking pots from the Goddess Durga and his adventures with the pots. Can be used for a study of art or a character study.

*Toye, William. (1969). *How summer came to Canada.* Illustrated by Elizabeth Cleaver. New York: Walck. [Canadian Indian]
When Indians were created Winter moved from his Far North home into Eastern Canada. Glooskap, creater of the Indians, goes south to find Queen Summer, captures her, and returns to his country. Summer overcomes winter and suggests a compromise. The rich, glowing colors of Elizabeth Cleaver's collage illustrations enhance the mood of the seasonal setting. This legend is recommended for reading to the class as an introduction to the importance of setting.

*Toye, William. (1977). *The loon's necklace*. Illustrated by Elizabeth Cleaver.
     Toronto: Oxford University Press. [Canadian Indian]
A Canadian legend of a blind man whose sight is restored by the loon who leads him
into the lake. The man throws his shell necklace to the bird and the beads become
the white markings on the black loon feathers. Compare with "The Blind Boy and
the Loon" retold by Ramona Maher, and with the film produced by the Encyclopedia Britannica Educational Corporation. In the film version the man saves
the whole tribe from starving, not just his family, and the shell necklace is more than
a prized belonging, holding meaning as a medicine man's tradition.

*Toye, William. (1969). *The mountain goats of Temlaham*. Illustrated by Elizabeth
     Cleaver. New York: Walck. [Canadian Indian]
This legend is beautifully illustrated with brilliant collage displaying Indian designs
and totems. The law of the hunt from old times was to kill only what was needed for
meat and skin and antlers. The legend deals with the consequences of disregarding
the law. Characters are revealed through action and description, with little dialogue.
A comparison with the same tale told in *The Blind Boy and the Loon and Other Eskimo
Myths* by Ramona Maher demonstrates the difference in the amount of information
given about the character and the need for drawing conclusions.

*Vinci, Leonardo da. (1973). *Fables of Leonardo da Vinci*. Collected by Bruno Nardini
     and illustrated by Adriana S. Mazza. Northbook, IL: Hubbard Press.
     [European]
Nardini collected these from Leonardo da Vinci's manuscripts. Nardini attributed
their origin to Leonardo, although in the past five centuries, tales in this collection
have circulated through storytellers in Italy and France. The message of the fable is
universal and fits today's society as well as the ancients'. Fine drawings complement
the tales.

Vuong, Lynette. (1982). *The brocaded slipper and other Vietnamese tales*. Illustrated by
     Vo-Dinh Mai. Reading, MA: Addison-Wesley. [Vietnamese]
Counterparts to the familiar European fairy tales are translated in this carefully
documented collection. Tam, in "The Brocaded Slipper," is a Cinderella character.
Little Finger, in "Little Finger of the Watermelon Patch," shares characteristics of
Thumbelina. Tu Thuc, in "The Fairy Grotto," reminds the reader of Rip Van Win-
kle. "Master Frog" had to work much harder than the frog prince to gain his real
identity. Quynh, an Eastern fairy princess, is similar to the Goose Girl. A comparison of these Vietnamese tales and their Western counterparts demonstrates the
unique individuality of each culture, and also the bonds of common humanity.

*Whitney, Thomas P. (1972). *In a certain kingdom*. Illustrated by Dieter Lange. New
     York: Macmillan. [Russian]
An interesting collection of Russian fairy tales that could be compared with other
translators' versions of the same story and with certain tales from other countries.

"The Firebird and Vassilisa" can be compared with Zvorykin's "The Firebird," "The Frog Princess" with the Chinese "Black heart of Indri." "The Wonder Working Steeds" and "Marya Moryevna" can be compared with tales from other countries with the theme of breaking taboos, such as the Eskimo "Moon Husband" or the Indian "Winter Wife."

*Whitney, Thomas P. (1968). *The story of Prince Ivan, the firebird, and the gray wolf.* Illustrated by Nonny Hogrogian. New York: Scribner's. [Russian]
In Whitney's version of the classical Russian tale, Prince Ivan's fate contrasts with that in Zvorykin's *Firebird.* Here he is raised from the dead by "water dead" and "water living." The beautiful flow of language and figurative expressions are worthy of note.

*Yagawa, Sumiko. (1981). *The crane wife.* Translated from Japanese by Katherine Paterson and illustrated by Suekichi Akaba. New York: Morrow. [Japanese]
Poetical, classical language marks this version of the ancient transformation tale. When Yohei breaks his word to his beautiful, mysterious wife, he loses her forever. The illustrations follow a traditional technique of Japanese painting in which various shades of water-thinned ink are laid on paper with soft brush strokes in delicate shadings. This most-loved folktale has been made into plays, movies, and an opera in Japan.

*Young, Ed. (1978). *The terrible Nung Gwama.* New York: Wm. Collins & World. [Chinese]
On the way to bring cakes to her venerable parents, a young woman meets the Nung Gwama, who promises to return that night to eat her. As she sits crying, pondering her fate, she is given weapons by many passersby. How will they work? Will they be enough to destroy the monster? Predicting the outcome as the story unravels, the reader can see the need to suspend judgment until the end. The illustrations, each a fan-shaped album leaf, present unique impressionistic versions of traditional Chinese art forms.

*Zemach, Harve. (1973). *Duffy and the devil.* Illustrated by Margot Zemach. New York: Farrar, Straus & Giroux. [English]
A Cornish tale retold, similar to Rumpelstiltskin, in which a devil agrees to help Duffy, a lazy and clumsy hired girl, do her spinning and knitting for three years. A mixture of original Old Cornish dialect with modern English highlights the text as the old housekeeper helps Duffy by luring the Squire to the devil's hideaway. The illustrations contribute effectively to the character portrayal.

*Zemach, Harve. (1965). *Salt: A Russian tale.* Illustrated by Margot Zemach. Chicago: Follett. [Russian]

This traditional tale tells of a merchant with three sons who seek their fortune with their father's ships. The youngest foolish brother is the hero of the tale. The amusing figures of speech and rich use of language make the story a delight to read.

*Zvorykin, Boris, & Onassis, J. (1978). *The firebird.* New York: Viking Press. [Russian]

Zvorkyin presented this exquisitely illustrated volume of Russian tales to France in gratitude for his new life there. The English translation, edited by Jacqueline Onassis, follows classic versions of the tales. The high adventure of Prince Ivan in search of a firebird can be read aloud with a background of ballet music. While universal elements of the quest are apparent, the setting is distinctly Russian.

References

Applebee, A. N. (1978). *The child's concept of story.* Chicago: University of Chicago Press.

Asimov, I. (1961). *Words from the myths.* Boston: Houghton Mifflin.

Bauer, C. F. (1977). *Handbook for storytellers.* Chicago: American Library Association.

Bettelheim, B. (1976). *The uses of enchantment.* New York: Knopf.

Blatt, G., & Cunningham, J. (1981). *It's your move.* New York: Teachers College Press.

Bosma, Bette. (1981). *An experimental study to determine the feasibility of using folk literature to teach select critical reading skills to sixth graders.* Ph.D. dissertation, Michigan State University, East Lansing.

Chapman, L. (1984). *Discover art* (Vols. 1–6). Worcester, MA: Davis.

Elkind, S. (1975). *Improvisation handbook.* Glenview, IL: Scott Foresman.

Fijan, C., & Fijan, E. (1973). *Making puppets come alive.* New York: Taplinger.

Galdone, P. (1961). *The house that Jack built.* New York: McGraw-Hill.

Graves, D. (1983). *Writing: Teachers and children at work.* Portsmouth, NH: Heinemann Educational.

Grimm, J. & W. (1980). *Hansel and Gretel.* Illustrated by Susan Jeffers. New York: Dial Press.

Isaacson, R., & Bogart, G. (Eds.). (1981). *Children's catalog* (14th ed.). New York: H. W. Wilson.

Johnson, P. (1964). *Paper sculpture.* Seattle: University of Washington Press.

Kipling, R. (1972). *Just so stories.* Illustrated by Etienne Delessert. New York: Doubleday.

Laliberte, N., & Mogelon, A. (1973). *Masks, face coverings, and headgear.* New York: Van Nostrand Reinhold.

Latshaw, G. (1978). *The theatre student and puppetry: The ultimate disguise.* New York: Richards Rosen Press.

Leach, M., & Freed, J. (1949). *Standard dictionary of folklore, mythology, and legend.* New York: Funk & Wagnalls.

Lobel, A. (1981). *Fables.* New York: Harper & Row.

Loon's necklace, The. (1981). [Film]. Chicago: Encyclopedia Britannica Educational Corp.

McDermott, G. (Producer), & Wichenhagen, I. (Director). (1975). *The stonecutter.* [Film]. Weston, CT: Weston Woods Studios.

MacDonald, M. R. (1979). *An analysis of children's folktale collections with an accompanying motif index of juvenile folktale collections.* Ph.D. dissertation, Indiana University, Bloomington.

MacDonald, M. R. (1982). *The storyteller's sourcebook: A subject, title, and motif index to folklore collections for children.* Detroit, MI: Heal-Schuman.

MacDonald, M. R. (1985). *Twenty tellable tales.* New York: H. W. Wilson.

Opie, I., & Opie, P. (1974). *The classic fairy tale.* London: Oxford University Press.

Reflections: A Japanese folktale. (1975). [Film]. Chicago: Encyclopedia Britannica Educational Corp.

Riordan, J. (1984). *Favorite stories of the ballet.* Illustrated by Victor Ambrus. Chicago: Rand McNally.

Rosenblatt, L. (1978). *The reader, the text, and the poem.* Carbondale: Southern Illinois University Press.

Rosenblatt, L. (1983). The reading transaction: What for? In R. Parker & F. Davis (Eds.); *Developing literacy: Young children's use of language.* (pp. 118–135). Newark, DE: International Reading Association.

Ross, R. (1982). *Storyteller.* Columbus, OH: Charles E. Merrill.

Schonewolf, H. (1968). *Play with light and shadow.* New York: Van Nostrand Reinhold.

Sloyer, S. (1982). *Reader's theatre: Story dramatization in the classroom.* Urbana, IL: National Council of Teachers of English.

Smith, F. (1978). *Understanding reading* (2d. ed.). New York: Holt, Rinehart & Winston.

Smith, F. (1982). *Writing and the writer.* New York: Holt, Rinehart & Winston.

Stauffer, R. G. (1980). *The language-experience approach to the teaching of reading.* (2d ed.). New York: Harper & Row.

Stewig, J. W. (1983). *Informal drama in the elementary language arts program.* New York: Teachers College Press.

Thompson, S. (1955–58). *Motif-index of folk literature* (Vols. 1–6). Bloomington: Indiana University Press.

Wilde, O. (1968). *The selfish giant.* Illustrated by Gertrude & Walter Reiner. New York: Harvey.

Yolen, J. (1974). *The girl who cried flowers and other tales.* New York: Thomas Y. Crowell.

Author, Title, and Illustrator Index

Subject Index